Praise for *Barefoot Tribe*

"*Barefoot Tribe* is a call to rediscover Jesus and His way in a manner that will change the world—as it always has. Palmer's writing is as clear as it is compelling, and convicting in the best sense of that word. After reading his book, I have decided to take off my shoes and join the tribe."

—John Ortberg, bestselling author, *Who Is This Man?*; senior pastor, Menlo Park Presbyterian Church

"Nothing great for God happens without passion, and you can feel Palmer Chinchen's passion on every page of this rallying cry for the church. Far from the usual diatribe on the church's impairments and plights, *Barefoot Tribe* is a call to arms toward a new kind of tribe that hears the cries of the world in everyday life and responds with passion to its hurts. The author's vision is not a church in pain but one that feels the pain of the world and salves its wounds. Chinchen changes each word of 'Here I Stand' to 'There We Go.' Painstaking and passionate, *Barefoot Tribe* shows us how to 'Take a Hike.'"

—Leonard Sweet, bestselling author, *The Gospel According to Starbucks*; professor, Drew University, George Fox University; and chief contributor to sermons.com

"Palmer Chinchen is a prophet to our generation, and *Barefoot Tribe* is his call to all who have ears to hear. Through fluid prose and captivating stories, Chinchen illuminates the true work of transformation and freedom for which we were all born. *Barefoot Tribe* is as much a movement as a manifesto, drawing us back to the heart of the Christ whose name we bear. A must-read for all who would follow the Way of the Master. Bravo! May we all heed its beautiful and haunting call."

—Ted Dekker, *New York Times* bestselling author

"Palmer is a modern-day prophet. In this manifesto, he delivers an impassioned challenge to live like Jesus, love like Jesus, and to be—not just go to—the church that our Savior founded with His own blood. If you want comfort and confirmation, then don't read this book. But if you want to be confronted and stirred up, then you can't afford to pass up *Barefoot Tribe*. Let's get back to heart of the gospel. Let's take pieces of heaven to places of hell on earth. Let's join the tribe!"

—Preston M. Sprinkle, author, *Fight, Charis,* and *Erasing Hell*; director of Eternity Bible College's Boise extension site

"Palmer helped me to imagine a world where the reality of the kingdom is evident in the followers of the King. He gives examples of where he sees followers of Jesus taking up the call to live selflessly, and he gives countless practical areas for me to do so as well. He does all of this in a way that disarms me of my cynicism and hesitancy to believe in the organized institutions that looked the other way on issues of compassion and justice. This book has helped me to dream again of a day when the righteous rise up from indifference, of a movement that is truly known by love—and after reading it I feel compelled, not by guilt, but by inspiration, to get involved."

—David Zach, Remedy Drive

"I've had the pleasure of calling Palmer a friend for years and can say that he truly lives these words. His passion is authentic and contagious. This manifesto was a game changer for my wife and me. It was as if the things God was impressing on our hearts was put into words. It's a message that we needed to hear and a message that I believe all of us in the church need to hear. I've never been more excited to be a part of the Tribe!"

—Josh Havens, lead singer of The Afters

"If you care about the world we live in, desire to positively impact this world, and have a faith that guides you, *Barefoot Tribe* is a must-read."

—Jay Feely, NFL Kicker,
2014 NFL Man of the Year Nominee

BAREFOOT
TRIBE

TAKE OFF YOUR SHOES AND DARE
TO LIVE THE EXTRAORDINARY LIFE

Palmer Chinchen, PhD

HOWARD BOOKS
A Division of Simon & Schuster, Inc.

New York   Nashville   London   Toronto   Sydney   New Delhi

HOWARD BOOKS
A Division of Simon & Schuster, Inc.
1230 Avenue of the Americas
New York, NY 10020

Also available in audiobook from Oasis Audio. www.oasisaudio.com

Cover photograph and interior photographs by Laine Sandoval
Cover graphics by Gil Sandoval
SANDOVAL PHOTOGRAPHY: www.sandovalphotography.net
SANDOVAL DESIGN: www.sandovaldesign.com

First Howard Books trade paperback edition September 2014

HOWARD and colophon are trademarks of Simon & Schuster, Inc.

For information about special discounts for bulk purchases, please contact Simon & Schuster Special Sales at 1-866-506-1949 or business@simonandschuster.com.

The Simon & Schuster Speakers Bureau can bring authors to your live event. For more information or to book an event, contact the Simon & Schuster Speakers Bureau at 1-866-248-3049 or visit our website at www.simonspeakers.com.

Designed by Davina Mock-Maniscalco

Manufactured in the United States of America

10   9   8   7   6   5   4   3   2   1

Library of Congress Cataloging-in-Publication Data

Chinchen, Palmer.
Barefoot tribe / Palmer Chinchen, PhD.
    pages   cm
1. Christianity—21st century. 2. Chinchen, Palmer. 3. Missions—Liberia. I. Title.
BR121.3.C393 2014
270.8'3—dc23   2013043033

ISBN 978-1-4767-6195-4
ISBN 978-1-4767-6201-2 (ebook)

*This book is dedicated to my parents,
still living in Africa, Jack and Nell Chinchen,
who moved our family deep into the Liberian jungle
many years ago to live among the Sapo tribe.*

Contents

TRIBAL PEOPLE

CHAPTER 1   Tribes   3
CHAPTER 2   The Barefoot Tribe   9
CHAPTER 3   Good News for Bare Feet   21
CHAPTER 4   A Tribal Kingdom   31

PASSIONS WORTH LIVING: A MANIFESTO

CHAPTER 5   WE WILL Stop Injustice   45
CHAPTER 6   WE WILL Embrace People of Every Race,
             Nationality, and Background   59
CHAPTER 7   WE WILL Become Social Entrepreneurs
             and Empower Fair Trade   77
CHAPTER 8   WE WILL Become Modern-Day
             Abolitionists   97
CHAPTER 9   WE WILL End Extreme Poverty   109
CHAPTER 10   WE WILL Stop the Spread of Pandemics   125
CHAPTER 11   WE WILL Put Down Our Weapons   139
CHAPTER 12   WE WILL Promote Sustainability and
             Care for the Environment   153
CHAPTER 13   WE WILL Live Simply   167
CHAPTER 14   WE WILL Create More Art and Make
             the World Beautiful   179
CHAPTER 15   WE WILL Love Like Christ—Always   195

CONCLUSION: JOIN THE TRIBE

             Acknowledgments   217
             Notes   219
             About the Author   225

TRIBAL PEOPLE

CHAPTER I
Tribes

I GREW UP IN THE SAPO tribe, the barefoot people of Liberia. As a kid, my home was a bamboo-mat house in the Sinoe jungle, the world's thickest rain forest. A single-engine Cessna dropped my family off when I was six years old. The bush roads did not reach our remote mission. We had no running water or flushing toilets. Our drinking water from the creek was boiled in the large black pot out back, and kerosene lanterns lit our home at night. I shared my bed with our pet chimpanzee Tarzan . . . and my friends ran barefoot.

On Sundays our family walked the steamy jungle paths

for hours under the tropical sun for my father to preach to faraway villagers in mud-built churches with thatched roofs. The children in the bush had never seen an American hiking though their jungle. Whenever they saw my twin brother and me they always cried the same warning, "*Yomplu!*" (meaning "white spirit"), then ran away.

In the jungle, shoes are the exception. That's why most of my friends had swollen stomachs or orange-colored hair.

Worms crawled in under the children's toenails with the mud and the dust. They multiplied in their small bodies and bloated their stomachs like aged alcoholics, or made it look as though they'd had too much to eat. But it was never food that swelled their bellies—it was always the worms.

Their hair turned orange because the worms robbed their bodies of the nutrition they needed to live. Their urine was always rust-colored, because the bilharzia parasites made them bleed on the inside as they were slowly eaten to death.

It's a disturbing fate. That's why my blood boiled recently when a student at a large Christian university found me after I finished speaking and suggested I stop taking shoes to Africa, "Because," he said, "Africans' feet grow tough, and they don't need the shoes."

His ignorance was astonishing . . . and offensive.

Shoes are a rare and valued treasure in the jungle. So I was surprised when a young Sapo girl gave hers away.

On a stifling, dry-season afternoon, our bamboo house in the bush caught fire. Out of breath after running from the burning house, I stood on the grass next to my sister, Lisa, watching our home burn with violent intensity. The air smelled like a lit match, only stronger. Lisa cried deep sobs. I didn't know someone could have so many tears. Then I noticed she had no shoes. Lisa had run out in such a hurry that she'd left her shoes in the burning house.

Her best friend, a Sapo girl named Sophie, was standing next to her. She, too, saw that Lisa had no shoes. So she knelt down, pulled the shoes off her feet, and gently slipped them onto Lisa's.

I was surprised by the act of generous love, but I shouldn't have been, because this is the way of the Sapo tribe.

———

TODAY, ANOTHER KIND of tribe is forming.

We are on the crest of an epic shift in humanity. As social theorist Jeremy Rifkin writes, "The Age of Reason is being eclipsed by the Age of Empathy."[1] This generation views the world as an extended family—increasingly interconnected through technology—and they live with a deep moral obligation to care for one another and a determination to change what is wrong in this world.

These innovative and impassioned millennials are convinced they are to be both in culture and shape culture. They are not waiting for governments, institutions, or large denominations to change what is not right in our world. They are acting on their own passions and empathy. They believe Jesus' kind of kingdom can be grown from small "mustard seeds"—not just through massively financed corporate or government efforts—if they collaborate to take action and risks to remake the world.

Their tribes unite around a cause, and because of their mass, they have the power and resources to initiate change and accomplish so much more than the individual could alone. They are not an organization or a business; they are not about making more money. They are about their common desires, sharing stories, supporting each other, and living on mission together.

The church must embrace this movement and harness this force, because the values are so richly biblical. After all, it was Jesus who said, "Whatever you did for the least of these, you did for me."[2] I challenge the dispassion of the church of decades past. It's time for a church that does not withdraw into the safe confines of its sanctuary walls, but rather is willing to reach out to bring about a new kind of world based upon kingdom values.

THIS BOOK IS an invitation. It is your invitation to join the tribe. A tribe of innovative Christ-followers who are passionate about justice, compassion, art, sustainability, simplicity, beauty, eradicating extreme poverty, stopping pandemics, and sharing the love of God.

This is your invitation to contribute, to give your most

passionate effort, to give this world all you've got . . . and to give heaven your best life on earth.

I hope you can see that God wants to use your life—your one and most valuable life—to shape and change this world for good.

CHAPTER 2
The Barefoot Tribe

TRIBES FORM IN EVERY REALM of life. Practically all people have been or are in a tribe. We have a tribal instinct to connect over common passions or pursuits. The brilliant entrepreneur Seth Godin writes, "Human beings can't help it; we need to belong. One of the most powerful of our survival mechanisms is to be part of a tribe, to contribute to (and take from) a group of like-minded people."[1]

Some tribes are closed to outsiders and filled with rules and regulations. Those are dying tribes. This book is about the kind of tribe that courageously embraces something new.

This kind of tribe is interested in creating change, sharing ideas that go viral, and inspiring movements.

The new millennium missional church is being shaped by God-passioned creatives and innovators who believe they can make the world better and more beautiful—we'll call it the *Barefoot Tribe*.

PEOPLE USED TO wait for large organizations or national personalities to give leadership and initiate change. We expected large denominations to set the course, or massive nonprofits and global missions organizations to lead the way, or nationally syndicated radio stations to play the music, or large music labels to sign the bands. But this generation has stopped waiting. They don't have patience for bureaucracy. They don't want to fund the layers of organizational charts. They are not interested in policy and polity. They want direct trade. They like the indie labels. They want 100 percent of their resources to reach the person in need.

This week the *End It* movement is running a social media campaign asking people to "shine a light on slavery" by writing a red X on their hands, taking selfies of the red X's, then posting them online. Their message is, "Tell your world that slavery still exists, and *you won't stand for it*. Use your influence any way you can to help us carry the message of freedom so even more people know." They are right. They have more than 92,000 likes and 11,631 people talking about the cause already.

I love the spirit of tribal millennials. They start nonprofits the way Starbucks opens stores. They pop up everywhere—sometimes even across the street from each other. But they have something people crave, so they keep building more.

You also have the tools at your fingertips, literally, to create a groundswell right now. In this new global climate, you are the impetus for change. You are the one who will inspire others. You have the ability to launch a start-up, NGO (nongovernmental organization), ministry, or nonprofit. With Facebook, blogging, Twitter, Pinterest, YouTube, and Instagram, you can motivate not just hundreds, but millions.

With a tribe, your influence is limitless.

TRIBAL VALUES

A TRIBE OF people formed on Facebook just last week wanting to make vital organs more accessible to desperate people in need of a transplant. In the first twenty-four hours more than five thousand people signed up as organ donors.

Tribal passion runs deep. Tribes have glue, because they hold a shared belief. Their common faith fills them with purpose and a sense of oneness. Like a college's football team taking the field as clear underdogs, they become one. They find a strength deep within. They play with passion that no individual will find on his or her own . . . and they win.

And that's the entire message of this book: when people

come together and work in unison, they have the strength to transform entire societies.

This is the power of the tribe:

The Tribe Collaborates

WHERE I LIVED in Africa, they say this in the tribe: "One man cannot lift a house." When a man is ready to build his family a new hut, he calls the people of the tribe together to make mud bricks. The clay is dug from the muddy edges of the swamp and carried in brick-shaped wooden hoppers from the pit to the home site, where the clay will dry before being stacked into a kiln and fired. The hoppers are toted with a jog, so the mud will settle and fit the mold. It's backbreaking, exhausting work. One man could never do it alone. One man cannot lift a house. However, when the tribe rallies and collaborates, they will do it in a day.

The Tribe Pools Its Resources

IN LIBERIA, WHEN your son is about to leave the village to attend high school, he will go hut to hut, sit down with each member of the tribe, and tell them of his exciting future. They know before the question is asked that they, too, must help with his school fees. He is not just the son of Wolo Kleebo. He is a son of the tribe. So the tribe must pool its resources to send him to school. And the entire tribe will celebrate his graduation.

The Tribe Cares

NO ONE HURTS alone in the tribe. When tragedy or sadness strikes, the tribe comes to you. They gather in your home. They don't ask permission to visit; they simply say, "I'm coming to you." And they will sit with you for hours. You don't have to say much. Their presence says it all—*I am with you on your dark night.*

The Tribe Is One

I LEARNED EARLY on in the jungle, nobody walks alone. The Sapo people always ask each other the same favor when they are about to leave: "Carry me halfway."

They say "carry me." They actually mean, "Walk with me. Come be with me. I don't want to walk alone, especially at night."

They say "halfway" just to be polite. No one ever walks only halfway—they always carry you home.

The Tribe Shares

SHARING IS WHAT the tribe does best. When the Marweahs, our neighbors who lived in the bamboo-mat house next to ours, planned to leave Sinoe for a year, the people of the tribe came to them one by one, asking, "What thing must I keep for you?" They knew the Marweahs could not take all their belongings with them. There are no storage units in the jungle. Liberians say, "I will keep it for you," but in reality we all know it's theirs for good. By the time the Marweahs left their home it was completely empty. Every bed, every chair, every sheet, every knife and fork had been given away. The tribe shares.

So the tribe collaborates, pools their resources and abilities, cares, encourages each other, shares everything, and walks the path of life together. It sounds a lot like the kind of tribe Jesus came to start.

IT COULD HAVE been the memory of generous love by the Sapo girl years ago that made me start carrying shoes back to Africa. Maybe it was the thought of all my friends in the bush whose feet festered from walking barefoot. Or it could have been from watching high school boys share their shoes on the soccer field so their friend could play with at least one shoe on. I think it was the pool of all these memories that made me begin taking suitcases of shoes to Africa each time I returned. I never seemed to have enough. That's why I finally told the people of The Grove (the church I help lead in Chandler, Arizona), "I need your help—I need your shoes."

A few years ago, we dubbed one Sunday "Barefoot Sunday." I hoped people would get the idea that each of us has the resources, means, and ability to make a difference in a hurting world. I asked everyone to come to church wearing their best and favorite shoes, then take them off and go home barefoot. Our team heading to Africa would pack their shoes and give them away.

I had never heard of a church anywhere trying something like this, but I was convinced that leaving church barefoot would help our people get that this world is a broken place. And understand the profound truth that *with your one and very important life you can change what is not right in this world*—if we will care less about things like shoes and care more about people who hurt.

That first Barefoot Sunday more than two thousand pairs of shoes were left on our stage, and the next year, five thousand pairs!

As news spread I began to receive emails from people and pastors as far away as Florida and Maryland to say they, too, were holding a Barefoot Sunday. A college in Ohio asked me to come speak on the day their entire student body walked barefoot in order to share their shoes. Surprisingly, a young reporter in Texas invited her entire city to go barefoot for Africa . . . and they did.

As I've traveled the country talking about the kind of missional life God calls us to live and watched Christ-followers across the country; from California to Florida, Illinois to Texas, take off their shoes and walk home barefoot, I sense a movement is swelling—a tribe is forming of people who actually want to live the gospel and spread the kingdom of heaven in places of hell on earth.

TWO THOUSAND YEARS ago, at a spring evening dinner for a few close friends, a young Jewish rabbi started a barefoot tribe—on a day we could call Barefoot Thursday. In the middle of the meal, the Christ abruptly stood to take off his coat and wrapped a towel around his waist.

The room went silent as Jesus bent down in front of his closest friends and, one by one, pulled off their shoes—then washed their bare feet. When the stubborn one resisted, Jesus calmly reminded Peter, "You cannot be a part of this kind of kingdom-movement until you take off your shoes."

When all the shoes were off and their feet washed, he said to them, "I, the Master and Teacher, washed your feet, you must now wash each other's feet. I've laid down a pattern for you. What I've done, you do . . . If you understand what I'm telling you, act like it—and live a blessed life."[2]

So what is this pattern? In what ways must we act? How can we live this most blessed life?

The answer is simple. Follow the *missio Dei* of the Christ, which he sums up by saying, "He has anointed me to bring good news to the poor. He has sent me to proclaim the captives will be released, that the blind will see, the oppressed will be set free."[3]

Next, he says to all who wish to join this tribal movement, live this way:

Feed the hungry,
Give clean water to the thirsty,
Build houses for the homeless,

Share your clothes when people are cold and your shoes
    with the barefoot,
Care for the sick and everyone with AIDS,
Become a voice for justice.[4]

Eleven young men came as followers. They left that
night as tribal leaders—ready to make the world better and
more beautiful. A tribe had formed; a movement had
begun.

————————

SINCE THE GROVE'S first Barefoot Sunday, a tribe *has*
formed, a movement begun.

Over the past two years, here's what has happened in our
tribe:

- The tribe partnered with coffee growers in
  Thailand to provide fair-trade coffee in Chandler.
  We call it "Tribal Coffee."

- Teams formed to rebuild an orphanage in Haiti.

- Junior-highers filled more than a hundred
  backpacks with school supplies for children of the
  Navajo tribe.

- The tribe rallied to repaint more than a hundred
  homes in blighted neighborhoods.

- The tribe rebuilt a girls' dorm in Liberia after the
  civil war.

- Tribal people began tutoring children of immigrants in the Phoenix East Valley.

- High-schoolers launched an effort to give away mosquito nets in Africa.

- The tribe sponsored 105 college students in Africa in one day.

- The tribe rallied their resources to dig four wells in Malawian villages to provide clean water.

- A motley band of tribal artists painted murals on city walls where Phoenix's homeless gather.

- And the tribe sent dirt bikers to Liberia to ride jungle trails and put twelve thousand pairs of shoes on bare feet.

In many ways, I think this gathering of God's people in Chandler at The Grove is now more a tribe than a church. I say that because somewhere in our Western practice of faith we have made the church more a place than a people. But this eclectic collection of passionate Christ-followers is committed to justice, sustainability, microeconomics, art, fair trade, compassion, generosity, and austerity.

I write this book because what is happening in Chandler is not staying in Chandler. As I travel the country telling people about this tribe, more want in. More tribes are forming and flourishing. The face of spirituality is changing.

This next generation of Christ-followers is ready to live differently. They wear Toms shoes, because Toms puts shoes on bare feet in places like Bolivia. They've made scooters cool again, because you can ride a hundred miles on a gallon of gas, which leads to fewer oil wells off the gulf coast of our southern cities. They embrace simplicity, because they want to share more with people who have less. They will pay more for their cup of coffee if it's fair-trade. They are living the way Jesus said to live when he pulled the shoes off a dozen people's feet and said, "Follow me." And here's what I know about you. God has planted a burning passion in your soul to change something that is wrong in this world. I know it's there. It's just that you don't think you have the resources, or the time, or the right background or experience to make it happen.

Somewhere in the back of your mind you believe someone else will act. Someone else will abolish the sex slave trade. Someone else will dig the well. Someone else will end the malaria.

But that *someone* is you.

You are the one called by God. God himself put you on this earth with a unique passion, special ability, fresh perspective. So give us all you've got. Give this world all you've got. Stop holding back.

The Christ left this work of bringing healing to a broken world to you and me. Oppression, injustice, poverty, bigotry, and abuse are real and present. But it doesn't have to be this way. When Jesus left, he asked that you and I continue to change and love the world.

If I can convince you of only one thing, let me convince you that *you* are the one who will do the most critical things for God. Not for fame. Not to be spectacular, but to make this world better and more beautiful.

Your time to act is now.

CHAPTER 3
Good News for Bare Feet

IT'S THE TROPHY HUNTERS OF Africa that got me.

I've spent about half my life in Africa, and I can't tell you how disenchanted I eventually began to feel about the trophy-hunting preachers. They came from faraway churches and mission organizations to preach to the Sapo tribe. And before they left, they always asked for a raising of the hands. Then they returned to their countries exclaiming about how many hands were raised.

But they missed it. They missed the rest of the gospel! They missed the part when Jesus said, "Care for them, feed them, love them, free them."[1]

I sat in evangelistic crusades in mud-brick churches with thatched roofs and listened to the trophy hunters implore people to come forward to be saved from hell. However, they never asked about the children sitting on the dirt floor with their swollen bellies and their infected toes that come with living barefoot. They never said a word about the hell on earth.

They ignored that part of carrying the good news.

You see, they came to take home a trophy, not to bring the kingdom of heaven to earth.

FOUNDATIONAL TO THIS book—and to becoming the kind of people God desires us to be—is a fresh understanding of *gospel* and *kingdom*. So before we explore the passions of tribal people, I want to take a few pages to explain what Jesus meant when he talked about gospel and kingdom.

THE GOSPEL PROBLEM

SOMEWHERE IN OUR land of evangelical traditionalism, image magnification, and hundred-million-dollar church buildings, we have lost sight of the kingdom life Jesus came to bring. We have been building kingdoms on street corners rather than spreading the infectious beauty and goodness of the kingdom of heaven on earth.

We've turned the gospel into a personal, intellectual

transaction with God that never affects the world in which we live. But the way we live matters, because the way we live every day is a picture of our souls.

You see, the gospel is not just about making it into heaven; it's about filling this world with the beauty and love of God. Living out the gospel means you leave the comfort of your manicured suburb, your polished shopping mall, your neighborhood Starbucks, and your place in the pew to make heaven alive on earth.

Living the gospel means putting an end to personal dispassion and dispassionate churches.

When you start to live this way, something transformational happens on the inside. Something good happens in this world. Something beautiful. Something a lot like heaven.

———

I HAD JUST finished my seminar, talking about how I was convinced we could help end three of Africa's most desperate problems—extreme poverty, pandemics, and the exploitation of women—when a youth pastor in the back of the auditorium raised his hand and asked, "How do you rank that?"

"How do I rank that?" I honestly had no idea what he meant.

"How do you rank meeting the needs of people against the need to tell them they are sinners?" he clarified. "Rank their priority."

My answer was simple: "Jesus never ranked those things, so neither will I."

If we do one without the other, we miss it.

When I read the Bible, it becomes surprisingly clear that on a number of occasions the Christ himself simply met the needs of hurting people . . . and that was good news. Jesus never conditioned his good news on a person's response to his message. When he was confronted with desperate people, he simply showed the love and mercy of God. For example, when the bleeding woman grabbed on for life, he stopped—and stopped the bleeding.[2] When the little girl lay dead on her bed, he took her hand and gave her life.[3] When lepers, covered in shame, begged him to take away their disease, he made them clean.[4]

Without question, I desire that God rescue the souls of marginalized people, but if I miss that often their first and immediate need is food, or a home, or medication, or dignity, or freedom, or love . . . then I miss the good news as Jesus embodied it.

I understand the need for our hearts and souls to turn toward God, but in many circumstances we simply must act. And we do not act in order to manipulate someone to a decision. We act because they are desperate. Period.

MY FAMILY MOVED to Africa when I was a first-grader.

From an early age I knew that missionaries preached. They invited evangelists to hold gospel crusades. They rode in small, shiny bush planes to remote posts to preach the gospel—then flew away after counting the raised hands.

But something always seemed lacking and amiss. I felt this for years.

Every friend I had in the bush growing up was African. I knew their needs well. In the afternoon, when we met to play soccer, practically every one of them wore a shirt or shorts that used to belong to me or my twin brother, Paul. Some lived in mud huts with thatched roofs. They slept on woven bamboo mats on the dirt floor, covered at night only by a thin *lappa*. They loved the feeling of our soft mattresses when they came to our home for sleepovers and slept in our flannel pajamas covered with pictures of cowboys and Indians.

In spite of the fact that American Christians had been coming to West Africa for a hundred years, little had changed for the people in the bush. Every one of my friends had bouts with malaria. Babies still died in my mother's arms from lockjaw and dengue fever. Seku went to school barefoot, Marcus lived with leprosy, and Thomas Klebo's brother died from the pinching gut.

The gospel appeared to be good news for after they died; it didn't seem to be good news for life in the jungle today.

Years later, after leaving the jungle, I became a pastor and began leading people back to Africa and to places like Cuba and Haiti. But I made our mission different from that of the missionaries I grew up among; I tried to make it more like Jesus' mission. I had this innate sense there was more to the gospel than only preaching about it.

So I made it our mission to change the world for good. We took carpenters to put zinc roofs on the mud huts of wid-

ows. We took doctors and nurses to treat the children weak
with malaria, along with thousands of mosquito nets to hang
over their beds at night. We took shipping containers full of
shoes to put on bare feet. We brought high school students
whose only jobs were to hold orphans. *And* we taught children Bible stories, *and* we held pastor-training seminars, *and*
our athletes shared their gospel stories.

Then I noticed this: people changed. The very people
who had traveled to these places far and away—they
changed. People who had attended church their entire lives
turned to me in the middle of a Malawian orphanage to say,
"Today I met Jesus."

Because it was then that the entire gospel of Jesus
Christ came alive.

RECLAIMING THE GOOD NEWS

ONE OF MY primary motivations in writing this book is to
reclaim the New Testament meaning of gospel, because I
believe the gospel has been compromised. It has been rede-
fined, minimized, and misrepresented.

Let's take a step back and examine the words *good news*
as Jesus spoke them and intended them to mean. "Gospel" is
the English transliteration of the Greek word *euengelion*.
The word *evangelism* also finds its roots in the Greek word
euangelion, which Latinized is *evangelium*.

About two thousand years ago Jesus was born, and the
kingdom of God took root. Around AD 30 this young rabbi

began traveling throughout the Galilee region proclaiming, "I have *euangelion* [good news]!" But the term was not original to the Nazarene rabbi. He was commandeering Caesar's language.[5]

In the first century, *euangelion* was a Roman Empire proclamation of great news. For example, when Caesar conquered an enemy, his emissaries would ride on horseback from village to village across his kingdom and stop in town centers to declare, "I have *euengelion*." Or, as another example, a messenger would proclaim, "Good news [*euengelion*], the empress has given birth to a son, an heir to the throne!"

Jesus' use of the term was brilliant. Everyone knew what he meant; he was offering better news than Caesar's. A better kingdom than Caesar's.

Jesus' good news of a different kingdom, however, was dangerous; it got him killed.

But he rose again! The movement went viral.

Followers of Christ were convinced this message had implications for the entire world. Their good news was not like Caesar's, which was about power and control and excess. Instead, this kingdom was about love, grace, acceptance, and justice. They saw the world was a broken place and things were not the way God meant them to be. The message of these new Christ-followers became one of repairing and reclaiming this world for God. God was ready to redeem his creation plan.

The gospel, then, is this: God's kingdom has come to a broken world, and God is reshaping the world with the help of his people.[6]

Through Jesus, God is doing something new. He is calling you—his followers—to be and do for the world what Israel was once called to be and do: to spread peace, love, dignity, healing, and hope, to be the ones proclaiming to the world the good news of life with God.

THE BEST NEWS is, the tribe gets it. They understand that living out the gospel means you become willing to leave the comfort of your sectional, your family, your gym, your place in the pew, and your adult Sunday school-class, to go to the ends of the earth—in pursuit of something better for hurting people.

They understand that God has something good for desperate people—all people. That our gospel message is about so much more than a single-moment decision. Rather, we are called to embody the gospel.

The gospel is not simply a proposition.

It's a way a life.

All my life, I've heard people say, "Preach the gospel." I can't remember ever hearing anyone say, "Live the gospel."

It is time for the rest of the church to recapture the New Testament gospel that is full, rich, and deep. Gabe Lyons, in *The Next Christians,* says we have truncated the gospel, created a Cliffs Notes version. In other words, we've grabbed on to the tip of the iceberg, believing all the while we hold the whole thing.

When Jesus talked about gospel—in the Gospels—he talked about a social revolution, of healing and repairing. The last would be first; the least would be the greatest.

I challenge you to expand your idea of "good news." Usually, we think of goodness in terms of what we do not do, rather than what we do.

For example, if I don't do certain things—smoke, drink, cuss, tell terrible lies, watch too much *Real Housewives of Orange County*—then I'm good.

I think the good of the Bible is far more proactive.

When Jesus healed ten lepers—that was good. When he gave a blind man sight—that was good. When he brought a boy in Nain back to life—that was good. When he stopped the bleeding of a dying woman—that was good. When he gave dignity to the woman who was "famous for her many sins"—that was really good.

THIS IS GOOD.

Keith is in Haiti right now. Keith first traveled to Haiti with me earlier this year to help rebuild a pastor's home and his church that collapsed in the earthquake. I was surprised Keith was willing to make the trip since not much earlier he had undergone surgery to give a friend one of his kidneys. While in Kenscoff, Keith met Melissa, a woman who leads after-school programs in several dozen of the countless orphanages in Port-au-Prince. When Melissa learned Keith taught high school theater, she pleaded with him to return and give drama lessons to her leaders. That's why Keith and his wife are back in Haiti this week.

When a man gives his kidney to a friend, that's good news. When you spend a week building pews and a podium for a newly rebuilt church on a mountain called Beautiful, that's good news. When a drama teacher helps orphans re-enact the Bible's stories and share them through theater, that's good news.

That's a lot of good news—all from one man named Keith.

CHAPTER 4
A Tribal Kingdom

I WAS IN FIRST GRADE, SIX years old, when my mother, who was about to pray with me before I went to bed, asked if I would like to accept Christ. I did. We knelt next to my bed and I prayed the prayer with her, and we excitedly told Dad.

That same year my family moved deep into the African jungle.

By age twelve, I had accepted Christ a dozen more times. The spiritual laws expert insisted we come forward when I was nine. He talked a lot about burning in hell, and a lake of fire, and gnashing teeth. He didn't have to say a lot more to persuade me to make the walk down front.

Then, lightning killed two friends. That's when I asked God into my heart another ten times, because I was certain I was a goner when the next tropical storm blew in.

My point is, I heard a lot about making it to heaven and escaping hell when I was a kid. However, in spite of the many missionaries in Africa, I can't remember once hearing that God's kingdom was present. The only thing I knew about his kingdom was that it was in heaven—and I lived in the hot, sweaty, malaria-infested, blood-diamond country of Liberia. I honestly thought I would never live long enough to graduate from high school. That is why I wanted to make sure I made it into heaven, not hell—when I died from a green mamba strike, a rebel soldier's bullet, or a bolt of lightning.

But the good news of the gospel being a catalyst for changing the current fate of the tribe? Not something I ever heard.

And that's the root of the problem; the kingdom of God is not being made tangible. In our Christian tradition, we have made the kingdom of God so spiritual, so internal, and so much about another life that it never affects the world we live in every day.

I was a pastor for years before I discovered the kingdom of God as Jesus described, and when I did, it became life-changing—exhilarating—eye-opening.

I had heard friends in ministry talk much about the kingdom, but I wasn't really sure what they meant until I was invited by Matt Hammett (who leads Flood Church in San Diego) and Chris Clark (my lifelong friend and founder of

Children of the Nations) to participate in a brainstorming session for emerging leaders. The sole purpose was to dream about the kingdom. What would it look like if churches across the country began to pool their resources and people and passions to spread the kingdom of heaven on earth?

About twenty of us gathered in a sprawling Southern California home that sat on a cliff's edge overlooking the deep-blue Pacific. The view was spectacular, the kingdom dreaming even more so. I had never, in all my years of ministry, or in all my life as a Christian, heard the kingdom of God talked about in such tangible, compelling, and inspiring ways.

I soaked up everything that was said. My appetite had been whetted. I wanted more. I went on a years-long quest to dig up and learn all I possibly could about Jesus and the kingdom-life he spoke of so often.

Then another friend in ministry told me to read English theologian N. T. Wright.[1] His fresh perspective on the kingdom of God was like finding a river in the desert. I stuck my head in and drank deeply. Next I stumbled on Scot McKnight's *One.Life.*[2] I couldn't put it down. I was dumbfounded by how much of the story of Christ and God I had missed.

The kingdom-world I discovered was revolutionary. It changed everything. It gave my life and ministry new meaning and impetus. The gospel made sense. The experience was energizing, life-giving, empowering. I felt as if I was entering an entirely new dimension of our spirituality.

LAST WEEK I hurried up to the US Airways kiosk, just outside of security, to print out my boarding pass. After I swiped my credit card for ID, the screen asked, "Would you like an upgrade?" *You bet I would.* I punched the yes button. As I grabbed my boarding pass, I did a double-take. I was in seat 3D. First class! Jackpot.

I had a hard time believing it was true. So after being groped by TSA I stopped at the first US Airways desk I came upon. "Could you look at my boarding pass? The machine just printed me a first-class ticket. Do you think it billed my credit card?" The agent looked at my boarding pass, then said with a warm smile, "No, honey, you've been upgraded."

You're darn right.

When I settled into my first-class seat I still felt there had to be a mistake. This had never happened before. Then, just when I started to sip on my ice-cold drink in a crystal goblet, someone blurted, "You're in my seat!"

What? I knew it. I pulled out my boarding pass to protest being relegated to coach. "Look, it says right here I'm in 3D." Pointing at the other seats I explained, "A, B, C, D. See, I'm in D."

"There is no C in first class," she snapped snarkily. "You're sitting in 3E, not 3D."

Whew, still in first.

Not long after takeoff I smelled something.

Now, I have spent thousands of hours in coach, and there's a smell in there, too. Kind of a junior high locker room smell. This was different; it was ravishing. It was ravioli, with fruit and cheeses on china.

As the flight attendant set my gourmet Italian dinner in front of me, I whispered, "You are an angel. You have no idea how much better this looks than the PB&J I have in my backpack." And I wasn't kidding.

A few minutes later, she brought dessert. Red velvet cake topped with whipped cream and chocolate flakes, floating on a bed of fudge.

It was a glorious flight.

As I reflect on my kingdom-discovery journey, I realize I have spent years in "Christian coach," when I could have been in first class. There is a whole world out there I never understood, never experienced, never entered into.

I had been the child C. S. Lewis writes about when he describes the limited life so many Christians live: "Like an ignorant child who wants to go on making mud pies in a slum because he cannot imagine what is meant by the offer of a holiday at the sea."[3]

I write this book for all of us who have missed the kingdom. I invite you to come inhale it. Absorb it. Soak in it. It's not too late. The kingdom of God waits for you.

YOUR KINGDOM COME . . . NOW

SPEAKING TO A crowd seated on the side of a hill, Jesus declared, "Your kingdom come, your will be done on earth as it is in heaven."[4] Then he made this intriguing statement: "The kingdom of God is at hand."[5] What did that mean? What does that mean for you and me?

When Jesus arrived on the scene, things were not well on the Israeli front. God had promised Abraham, "I will give you a land, and you will be a blessing to many nations!" However, by 37 BC, Rome had occupied all of Israel and the Jews had no land!

In the midst of their tumultuous domination by the Roman Empire, this rabbi began to preach, *I am bringing a new kingdom.* His words resonated with a desperate people. Then he began to tell them that his kingdom is for the dejected, the unemployed, the divorced, the broke, the lonely . . . and he told them they would sit at the top.

His words were dangerous but exhilarating.

A bit ridiculous.

There is a fundamental misconception today, however, regarding this kingdom of God.

Over the centuries, because people were unable to grasp the kingdom Jesus proclaimed, they began to teach, "You will enter the kingdom of God in another life, in another time—a place called heaven . . . after you die."

When Jesus talked about the kingdom, though, he always talked about it as an experience we are meant to live today, not something limited to our internal soul. It's not meant to remain cognitive; it's not only for another life in another realm. In every way it is meant to be tangible and now.

Don't get me wrong here. I believe heaven is for real, but I also believe Jesus' words about the kingdom are for today.

The great good news of the kingdom is that it is near; it starts now! When Jesus talked about the kingdom, it was imminent. That's why he said things like, "As you go, preach this message: The kingdom of God is near."[6]

When he opened his kingdom manifesto, he said:

> Blessed are you who are poor, for yours is the kingdom of God. Blessed are you who hunger now, for you will be satisfied. Blessed are you who weep now, for you will laugh. Blessed are you when people hate you, when they exclude you and insult you and reject your name as evil, because of the Son of Man.[7]

So the question is, are the poor only blessed after they die? Are the hungry only fed after they die? Do those who cry only laugh after they die? Are the excluded only accepted after they die? Do marriages only heal after we die? Do fathers and sons only reconcile and speak again after they die?

Or, do we believe Jesus when he says, "Now . . ."?

THE MAGIC KINGDOM

IF YOU ARE still not sure what I mean when I say *the kingdom of God is an experience meant to be lived,* maybe this will help. Let me share an allegory.

In recent years the people of The Grove, where I pastor, have partnered with a Chechewa tribal village in Malawi called Chimpampha. Consider what would happen if we decided we wanted the children of Chimpampha to know about a place called the Magic Kingdom.

We would gather teachers to travel to Chimpampha and

begin holding daily classes for the children. We'd have them memorize Magic Kingdom slogans, like "The happiest place on earth!" Then we'd teach them Magic Kingdom songs like "It's a Small World." We might bring in experts to explain the Magic Kingdom experience. Culinarians would describe the taste of funnel cake and talk about how the powdered sugar melts in your mouth. Physicists would put formulas on the chalkboard to explain how mass, velocity, and volume conspire to make your stomach feel like it's in your throat when your chair drops out from under you on the Tower of Terror. We would try to help the kids understand that Mickey and Minnie are nice rats, except the only rats the children know are the rats that bite their toes at night when they sleep on bamboo mats on the dirt floors of their mud huts with the thatched roofs. We might try to explain the Pirates of the Caribbean, but the ideas of swashbuckling and mutiny would seem lost on children trapped in a landlocked country who have never seen the sea.

Let's say we hold these classes for a year. Let me ask you this: at the end of a year how much will the children know about the Magic Kingdom?

Barely a whiff.

But what if we did this? Let's say we chartered a Boeing 747 and flew it to Malawi, then took a couple of huge buses to Chimpampha and told the children, "We're going to the Magic Kingdom!" We braid the girls' hair and tie in pink ribbons, slip new shoes on their feet, and give them frilly dresses. Then we give brightly colored Converse and crisp khakis to the boys.

Then they all pile into our 747 and fly to LAX. From

there we whisk them off to the Magic Kingdom. When they walk through the gates we hand each child a funnel cake and rush them with a Fast-Pass to ride the Matterhorn, where they screech with joy while powdered sugar blows all over their smiling faces.

Now do you think they know what the Magic Kingdom is all about?

OF COURSE, THIS is only an allegory. I am not saying you must fly children from Africa to Disneyland.

But, because the kingdom of God is an experience we are to live, The Grove has two Malawian interns living in Lilongwe, Richard Maguire and Blessings Chibambo, graduates of African Bible College. Richard and Blessings lead community development efforts in Chimpampha. They've formed a soccer squad to represent the village, started a system for church members to care for the town's widows, rallied the people to make mud bricks for a clinic, canvased the community with mosquito nets, begun leading a new sanitation and clean water program . . . *and* they pull the children together in the afternoons to teach them Bible stories, *and* they meet with the young men after soccer practice in the late afternoon for prayer and Bible study, *and* they invite college girls from African Bible College to teach the women's Bible study that meets under the towering baobab tree next to the mud-brick church . . . *and* they've put seven thousand pairs of shoes on bare feet.

I think the kingdom of heaven is coming to earth in Chimpampha.

LIVE THE KINGDOM

SOME WOULD SAY, of all Jesus' teachings, kingdom was his most central focus. His statements about kingdom are ripe with meaning and implication.

This new kingdom of the Christ is revolutionary in every sense. It is different from all other kingdoms. This kingdom expands when husbands and wives forgive. This kingdom grows when we love and accept people regardless of race or ethnicity. This kingdom spreads when people choose to show grace rather than anger. The kingdom of heaven comes to earth when love becomes the dominant value.

What if we actually took Jesus' kingdom manifesto seriously and started building hospitals to heal, digging wells to give clean water, building houses for widows, and treating immigrants (the Samaritans of our day) with respect?

What if we became famous for our grace, our AIDS clinics, our acceptance, our mosquito nets in Africa, our pervasive love, and our friendships with foreigners? What if we were famous for that? What if our most defining mark as Christians became this incessant love that characterizes kingdom living?

What would our world be like now?

PASSIONS WORTH LIVING: A MANIFESTO

SOME PASSIONS ARE WORTH GIVING your life to. For this new Barefoot Tribe I have written a manifesto listing passions worth living . . . and dying for.

- WE WILL stop injustice.
- WE WILL embrace people of every race, nationality, and background.
- WE WILL become social entrepreneurs and empower fair trade.
- WE WILL become modern-day abolitionists.
- WE WILL end extreme poverty.
- WE WILL stop the spread of pandemics.
- WE WILL put down our weapons.
- WE WILL promote sustainability and care for the environment.
- WE WILL live simply.
- WE WILL create more art and make the world beautiful.
- WE WILL love like Christ—always.

Over the next eleven chapters we will unpack each of these statements and explore the ways we can live, and take action, and finally become the kind of church (Christ-followers everywhere) Jesus originally called us to be.

CHAPTER 5
We Will Stop Injustice

A RRÊT! STOP!" I SHOUTED AT our driver when I saw a man with a branch beating a woman.

The rubble from the earthquake was still on the ground in Haiti. For more than a week, two dozen of us had been helping a pastor put the pieces of his home and life back together. Now we were returning to Port-au-Prince.

Our driver hit the brakes and we were almost to a stop, so I grabbed the door handle to jump out and hopefully stop the madness. Suddenly, our driver accelerated again. I don't know why.

From the backseat of our crowded four-door pickup, I

yelled, "*Arrêt!*" a couple more times . . . but he just kept driving.

For the next mile or so I debated whether or not I should insist he turn around and go back, but the traffic was heavy and the road was narrow . . . so I sat in silence.

As I lay in my cot that night the scene kept replaying in my mind. I felt all this anger toward the man beating the woman with the branch. Worse, I felt anger toward myself for not insisting we turn back and put a stop to the woman's pain and shame.

But it was too late. Far too late.

The moment to act had passed.

I share this to say that when you see the things that are wrong in this world, the time to act is now—today. The moment passes so quickly, like a fleeting glance out a window. When we remain seated in silence, we become numb and callous to the injustice. We end up living comfortably with our inaction and dispassion.

This next tribe of Christ-followers, on the other hand, is not okay with the silence that condones poverty and injustice. They are speaking up and taking action.

HEAVEN LOSES

I'VE BEEN WONDERING: why all the palaver lately about hell in the afterlife when hell already rages on planet earth?

The problem is, if we make hell in the afterlife, the only

demon we can remain anesthetized to is the hell right here, right now.

When Jesus was here he tried to wake us up to the fact that hell was already in front of us and what you did or did not do about it mattered for eternity. He told the story of a rich man and a beggar named Lazarus. Jesus says Lazarus was dirty and poor and the dogs licked his sores. And of all places, he lived just outside a gated community. A rich man on the inside saw the poor man every day, but the rich man was heartless, even though he was very religious. For him, hell was somewhere else, sometime after he died, not outside his gate.[1]

Yes, I believe in a real heaven and a real hell after we die, but Jesus' point in the story is that the most religious people often miss the fact that there is also a hell burning on earth. When we make our spirituality only a private, inner experience—distanced from the way we live every day—heaven loses.

And hell wins.

Like the man in Jesus' story, I can sit in my La-Z-Boy and watch *Keeping Up with the Kardashians* all the way from when I get home to bedtime and be completely at peace with my spirituality—never bothered by the man with the sores outside my gate—if my spirituality is only inner and personal.

If we make spirituality only about abstract theological ideas and spend our time pointing fingers and debating metaphysical realities we know little about, we miss it! All this theological banter empowers dispassion, and wasting our time and energy on hypothetical conjecture only keeps us from changing the way we live today and seeing what's outside our front doors.

And that's the hell in the whole thing. When we spend more time talking about the hell after we die and ignore the hell of six-year-old girls in Thailand being sold for sex, hell wins—and heaven loses.

UNSOCIAL JUSTICE

RECENTLY, SOMEONE AT church said to me, "You talk too much about social justice. Could you stop using that phrase here?"

What? I was dumbfounded. Where in the world would that kind of thinking come from?

Hell was winning.

I went home and scoured the Bible for every line I could find about justice, and the next Sunday, I read pages and pages of Scripture that spoke of God's demand for it.

I really don't get it when Christians say things like that. Why do we view justice with dubious suspicion? There is no reasonable way to disconnect justice from what it means to be a follower of Christ. The Bible is a book devoted to it, from the first pages to the last. It is filled with a mountain of statements about God's passion for justice and our responsibility to respond to injustice.

Here are some of my favorites:

The Torah

"Do not mistreat or oppress a foreigner, for you were foreigners in Egypt. Do not take advantage of a widow or an orphan." EXODUS 22:21–22

"Cursed is anyone who withholds justice from the foreigner." DEUTERONOMY 27:19

The Wisdom Books

"I rescued the poor who cried for help, and the fatherless who had none to assist them. . . . I made the widow's heart sing." JOB 29:12–13

"Evil people do not understand justice." PROVERBS 28:5

"Speak up for those who cannot speak up for themselves, for the rights of all who are destitute." PROVERBS 31:8

The Prophets

"Loose the chains of injustice and untie the cords of the yoke, to set the oppressed free . . . share your food with the hungry." ISAIAH 58:6–7

"He has shown all you people what is good. And what

does the Lord require of you? To act justly and to love mercy and to walk humbly with your God." MICAH 6:8

The Gospels

"He has anointed me to bring good news to the poor. He has sent me to proclaim that captives will be released, that the blind will see, that the oppressed will be set free." LUKE 4:18

"Then the king will say . . . take your inheritance, the kingdom prepared for you since the creation of the world. For I was hungry and you gave me something to eat, I was thirsty and you gave me something to drink, I was a stranger and you invited me in, I needed clothes and you clothed me, I was sick and you looked after me, I was in prison and you came to visit me. . . . Truly I tell you, whatever you did for one of the least of these brothers and sisters of mine, you did for me." MATTHEW 25:34–37, 40

The Letters

"Pure and [true] religion in the sight of God the Father means caring for orphans and widows in their distress." JAMES 1:27

Justice is the raging heartbeat of the Bible. It's the ringing theme from Genesis to Revelation.

The truth is, we cannot separate Jesus from justice. If we do, we create a brand of Christianity that is an abomination to God himself.

Let's think about this: Why did Jesus come from heaven to earth?

Yes, Jesus came to die for and to forgive our sins.

Yes, there is a real hell, and heaven is for real.

Yes, God wants you to spend eternity with him.

But if you refuse to follow Jesus into the homes of the broken, you're following something, but you are not following the Jesus of the Bible.

Recently, much has been written about the crisis in perception of the evangelicals. My concern isn't so much with perception. My fear is that we have actually become a self-indulgent, complacent people. That's the real crisis.

My question is, how can we say we love God if we are dispassionate about the people he loves who are living in hell on earth? We can't. The true condition of a person's heart, Jesus teaches, is judged by whether or not we love the desperate and despised of this world. This is the issue he raised in Matthew 25 when he talked about who would end up in heaven or hell.

GENERATION JUSTICE

THE BAD NEWS is, the biblical idea of the gospel has become lost in many of our modern Western churches. The good news is the tribe gets it. This tribe of God-followers does not just talk about heaven, they live it. This tribe is changing the way the world and the church sees God, understands Jesus, and experiences the gospel.

I hear this next generation called everything from generation digital natives to generation Z. No one is really sure how to label them. I think I know—I'm convinced they should be named *generation justice*, because this is what they are most about.

Like no generation before, they are passionate about changing the world for good.

Jennifer, the reporter who invited her entire city to go barefoot, is one of them.

Jennifer says she stalked me on Facebook and Twitter until I finally responded to her messages about wanting an entire city to go barefoot. She's a young, twentysomething reporter in Texas who is convinced we live with too much excess and need to give more away.

She insisted I come to Texas on their Barefoot Sunday. I did, and I was stunned. She had inspired a whole community. More than twenty churches, four schools, and two colleges participated. Thousands of people took off their shoes as a commitment to live simply and share more.

Audacious . . . and awesome.

Every time I speak on a college campus and walk its sidewalks and hallways, I'm reminded of this generation's commitment to justice and compassion. Flyers and posters litter (in the best of ways) the walls and bulletin boards promoting the passions of their students.

I love the flyers a young woman named Christian posted at Point Loma University. Her ministry is called Beacon of Light. The flyers were simple but profound. They invited students to meet in her dorm kitchen on Wednesday afternoons to make PB&J sandwiches, then drive to downtown San Diego to give their sandwiches to hungry people. Christian is not waiting for somebody else to feed the hungry in her city; she does not believe the marginalized are for someone else to love.

Generation justice has heard the cry of the ancients like Micah and Amos and Isaiah, and they've started to live the words of Jesus. They have begun bringing Christ's kingdom to earth, just as it is in heaven.

HELL LOSES

MY FRIEND LEELAND once wrote song lyrics that included the line, "I will follow you into the homes of the broken." I think most Christians are willing to follow Jesus to church, but how many will actually follow him into the shantytowns, and the blighted neighborhoods, and the inner-city slums, and the villages, and into the homes of the broken?

At the Fifty-fourth National Prayer Breakfast in Washington, DC, Bono said, "The one thing we can all agree on is that God is with the vulnerable and the poor. God is in the slums and the cardboard boxes where the poor play house. God is in the silence of a mother who has infected her child with a virus that will end both their lives. God is in the cries heard under the rubble of a war. God is in the debris of wasted opportunity and lives. And God is with us if we are with them."[2]

God is with us if we are with them . . . Let that sink in. So the question is this: Will you go where God is? Will you follow God to where he already is?

Maybe right now you're wondering, why is Palmer taking his theology from a rock star? Here's my question to you: why are some rock stars preaching better theology than some preachers?

I mentioned in a previous work that we can learn from the examples of Sean Penn and Angelina Jolie. Some have told me they are bothered that I would tell Christians to follow the example of movie stars.

You see, after the tragic earthquake in Haiti, Sean Penn moved to Port-au-Prince and built a tent city for forty thousand homeless Haitians. And Angelina Jolie has twice flown to Africa to bring destitute, motherless orphans home as her children.

So here's what I wonder: why are some movie stars living better theology than some Christians? That's what bothers me.

If Christ calls you to be one with the least and the last, are you following him into the homes of the broken? Because God measures your faith by how you treat orphans, widows, the poor, and foreigners. You cannot separate your spirituality from what you do, or do not do, about hell on earth.

Not long ago, I invited Leeland and his band to play "Follow You" on a Sunday morning at The Grove. It was no coincidence this was our annual Barefoot Sunday.

Before inviting people forward, however, I told them about bilharzia in Malawi. Bilharzia is a slow and deliberate killer, a patient and efficient parasitic worm. When a person with bilharzia urinates, some of the parasites leave their body in the urine, then wait in the dirt or the mud for days until a barefoot person steps in it. The parasite enters the person's body by lodging under the toenails or in an abrasion on the foot. Then it settles in the kidney or liver and reproduces by the thousands each day, slowly destroying the organ.

When I lived in Malawi, a team of researchers came through studying the pervasiveness of the parasitic disease. The researchers traveled from village to village studying the effects. One of their research tools was two jars of urine. In one jar, the urine was bright yellow and translucent, much like the urine you've seen your entire life. In the second jar it was dark, opaque, and rust-colored, tainted by blood.

The researchers would show the two jars to the village

children and ask, "Which color is your urine supposed to be?" Almost every single child pointed to the rust-colored urine. That was all they had ever known.

The children were slowly bleeding to death from the inside . . . simply because they walked barefoot.

Scripture has always made a connection between walking barefoot and oppression. When the Israelites, for example, were forced into slavery by Pharaoh, they worked barefoot under great affliction in Egypt. The Hebrew word for walking barefoot is *yahef*, "to be without shoes." At its core, the word implies that a person is deprived or left wanting.

I see a pattern: when God sends someone like Moses to free the oppressed, he asks them to take off their shoes. I think in part God wanted Moses to be with the slaves who walked barefoot. I think God wanted him to know just a bit of what it's like to walk as a slave—in the shame, the humiliation, and dehumanization. And I believe God wanted Moses to know when he gave his life to freeing slaves, he was walking holy ground with God.

So that Sunday I told our people, "If you are willing to follow Jesus Christ into the homes of the broken, then take off your shoes, bring them to the front, and place them on the stage as your 'I will follow you' statement."

God wants your life, not just your shoes.

God wants you to live bothered by what is not right in this world. He wants you to take a piece of heaven to the places of hell on earth.

On that Sunday people left more than five thousand pairs of shoes at The Grove.

When you take off your shoes to follow Jesus,
hell loses
and
heaven wins.

CHAPTER 6

We Will Embrace People of Every Race, Nationality, and Background

THE CIVIL WAR WAS OVER, and Liberia was slowly regaining its equilibrium. I had been flying all day across the continent and finally landed in Monrovia at sunset. I was hot, tired, and hungry.

A sweet Liberian named Nellie welcomed me to the gritty guest house by the beach and told me she had made arrangements for me to have dinner at the house down the dirt road where the Americans who worked for a large nonprofit stayed.

Great plan, because, like I said, I was famished.

Watching the amber African sun dip into the navy blue

Atlantic, I made the short walk down the dusty road along the beach to the American people's house. The blue and white concrete building looked ominous: razor wire, iron gate, and a watchman with a machete. Everyone in Liberia was still on edge as the country cooled after nineteen years of bloodshed.

After the guard with the machete finally let me pass I knocked on the heavy door. A late-twentysomething American man answered. He looked East Coast educated, dressed like a grad student on his way to the coffee shop.

"Here for dinner," I said, smiling.

"Say again?" he asked, noticeably confused by my presence.

"Nellie at the guest house said I should come here for dinner," I answered, just a bit crisply.

"Don't know anything about that," he answered, with little concern. "There's no dinner here for you."

The smell of food cooking in the kitchen leaked out the door with the ice-cold air-conditioning. I tried to explain that I had traveled all day, was tired, and had no way to get into Monrovia for dinner—and I was hungry.

He just kept shaking his head, "Like I said, there's no food for you here."

Eventually, he shut the door, and I heard the dead bolt fall into place.

It took a moment for it to sink in that I was rejected, excluded, left out . . . locked out.

Walking the dirt road back under a darkening sky, the shame burned more than my empty stomach.

JESUS' KIND OF TABLES

I GET THE feeling Jesus loved dinners and dinner tables. Some of his most memorable moments happened over food and around a table.

Tables are a powerful place of intimacy, but they can also be a painful place of exclusion, as I learned.

Life divided at the tables in Jesus' world. Meals were sacred, spiritual . . . and segregated. Dinners and banquets were not places to mix and mingle with the foreigner and the sinner. That's why Jesus' self-invited luncheon at the home of a notorious sinner like Zacchaeus was so unnerving for the pious Jew.

Whenever Jesus talked about dinner parties and banquets, though, they were for everyone. He said things like, "Go to the country roads. Whoever you find, drag them in. I want my house full!"[1]

He was done with all the separation and exclusion and judging, and he flung the gates of the kingdom open wide.

DOWN THE ROAD in the town of Queen Creek a high-schooler named Chy told her mom the kids were mocking her at lunch. She sat alone, but they still taunted from a distance. Some students even threw their trash at her.

Chy's mother knew her daughter's disability made it hard for her to make friends, but this abuse at lunch was too much. She picked up the phone and made a call, not to the school's administrators or any other authority. She called Carson, the quarterback of the football team.

When Carson heard how Chy was being treated at lunch, all he said was, "Don't worry, Mrs. Johnson, it won't happen anymore."

The next day Carson, with about half a dozen of his teammates, joined Chy at her table. They chatted with her, ate with her, invited her to their next game . . . and no one threw trash at Chy that day. The mocking stopped.

Chy's new friends now walk her to class, and she cheers from the stands at their games.

Everything changed for Chy around a lunch table, when a few football players sat down and shared a meal.

———

FOR DECADES, SOME HIGH schools in Georgia have held racially segregated proms. One for whites and one for blacks. I find it absolutely shocking that segregation is still alive at all in our country.

But last spring, students at one high school began to end this kind of racism.

When best friends Stephanie, Quanesha, and Keela realized they would not be allowed to attend their senior prom together, they decided they'd had enough and began planning their own prom. A prom for everyone—an integrated prom.

They were done with the absurdity of their southern school's tradition. Earlier in the school year, for the first time, the administration had allowed a racially diverse home-coming court. Quanesha was crowned queen, but then was banned from attending the white-only homecoming dance!

Senior Mareshia Rucker joined the planning for prom and led a team of students to organize the event and raise money. They started on Facebook, promoting their inte-grated prom, proudly writing, "We live in rural south Geor-gia, where not too many things change. Well, as a group of adamant high school seniors, we want to make a difference in our community. For the first time in the history of our county, we plan to have an integrated prom." Their cover-page banner read Love Has No Color.

I hit *like*.

They encountered some backlash in their southern rural community and found a few of their posters ripped down, but the planning continued.

That April, students of every race and background fanned out in couples and groups across the small town for dinner, then met at the community clubhouse for the dance.

One student said, "I feel like we are living Martin Luther King's dream."[2]

She is.

They are.

THE BAD NEWS is, all this segregation and discrimination and exclusion we feel in high school does not always end with a diploma. This same separation creeps into neighborhoods and workplaces and golf clubs . . . and churches.

I almost choked on my coffee when I read a *HuffPo* article recently about a couple being banned from the communion table at their small Kentucky church—because she was white and he was black.

I had to read the piece twice to believe it. This wasn't some kind of *National Enquirer* tabloid farce. This wasn't a news piece from 1950. This was right now.

The sheer madness of this behavior in a church should cause all of us who call ourselves Christians to cry out against such shameful discrimination and put an end to that kind of church.

Because that kind of church has nothing to do with Jesus' kind of church.

In the Jesus kind of church, love and acceptance dominate. In the Jesus kind of church, lines between races and nationalities and social statuses are erased. In the Jesus kind of church everyone is invited to the table.

In the book of Matthew, Jesus is frank about the kind of life that pleases God: "I was a stranger and you invited me in."[3]

He often reminds us that there is nothing exceptional about loving people like us, people who think, look, dress, live just like us—that's easy. What is difficult is opening our homes, churches, and lives to those who are dramatically different.

Jesus shows us a brand of love, a kind of church that transcends race, nationality, position, background, ethnicity, or any other factor.

When I say this I think of the way Jesus embraced the Samaritans, the ethnic dogs of his day. He spent time, for example, with the Samaritan woman by the well who was different from him in every way: dressed different, spoke different, looked different, believed different. His friends, we read, were shocked by his amiable acceptance of the Samaritan.

———————

C. S. LEWIS writes about how life can separate like the rings of an onion. You peel back one layer only to find another inner ring, and you are still on the outside. All of us know the ache of being left on the outside . . . and the power of being invited in.

Maybe you've had that moment when you arrive at a friend's Christmas party and quickly realize you know no one except the host, who is desperately busy. Everyone else seems to know someone. They stand in tight circles laughing and seeming to have compelling conversations.

But you know no one. So you fill a red party cup with a drink and start to nurse it and hold it close like it's the most interesting thing in the world, praying that someone will talk to you.

Then you notice a stranger walking your way. *Will he ask why I'm here? Does he want me to leave?* You know your thoughts are nonsense, but you're so insecure because all you have is the red plastic cup.

But he smiles, then introduces himself and asks your

name and chats. Soon he says, "Come with me; let me intro-
duce you to a few friends." And he walks you across the
room and widens a circle of friends and says, "Hey, everyone,
this is my friend Bob, and he's the most interesting man in
the world."

The invitation in is not simply good, it's life-giving.

Once in a while in our church's lobby or courtyard, I'll
notice a circle of friends talking when someone they don't
know so well walks up. The person stands and waits for the
shoulders to part, for the invitation in. Every so often the circle never opens. Maybe they didn't see them. Maybe it's just
a mistake. But soon, the person outside the ring drops their
head and walks away.

The circles and rings in churches must be broken. We
need a new kind of church that opens its arms to everyone
who walks in longing to be wanted and welcomed and loved,
as they are by God. We need more churches that remember
God is for the least and the last, the left out and the outcast,
the sinner and the saint. As Jesus himself said about the
kind of people welcomed at his table, "Go out quickly into
the streets and alleys of the town and bring in the poor, the
crippled, the blind and the lame."[4]

THE TRIBE OF emerging Christ-followers today understands
that the church must include all people. They are drawn
to the other. They embrace diversity. They love a mosaic of

people in their coffee shops, at their dinner parties, and in their churches. The tribe gets it, that heaven has come to earth when people of every color and country gather to be one—one people living one life, together, for Christ and his kingdom.

Eugene Peterson writes that Jesus says, "Invite the misfits":

> The next time you put on a dinner, don't just invite your friends and family and rich neighbors; the kind of people who will return the favor. Invite some people who never get invited out, the misfits from the wrong side of the tracks. You'll be—and experience—a blessing.[5]

When I imagine the Jesus kind of church, the best kind of church, the kind of church I dream of here:

- I imagine people of every race and every ethnicity coming together as one.

- I imagine a place where single mothers and broken families feel they are home.

- I imagine a community that cares for each other, rallying to pay each other's rent and repairing each other's broken cars.

- I imagine a family whose members accept and love each other, in spite of their flaws and baggage, past mistakes and raggedness.

- I imagine being safe among friends who only wish the best for me.

- I imagine Jesus walking among us, saying, "Well done, well done."

Rachel Held Evans says we need bigger banquet tables.[6] Tables that will seat people from every tribe and nation. That's why in our new worship space at The Grove we're putting in huge, heavy wooden tables for people from every place and background to sit together as one. And this is the reason this past Sunday we held a "Bigger Banquet Tables" event. We encouraged everyone to invite their neighbors and coworkers and anyone who needed to have dinner with friends. The plan was to sit everyone at *one* table. A table where everyone was included and no one was left out.

Five hundred and eighty people signed up. So we built a massive table that stretched six hundred feet (that's two football fields) through our pistachio grove, strung white Christmas lights through the branches overhead, and lit a forest of candles on the endless table.

The table was like nothing anyone had ever seen. It was so long you literally could not see the other end. An hour and a half before the banquet our Serve the World Pastor (and head chef for the night), Paul, in a moment of panic, whispered to me, "We will never fill this table! There's no way this many people will show up for dinner."

I said I thought they would come. But I certainly had my doubts. It was simply too great a banquet to fathom.

His response was, "If we fill this table, I'll eat my shoe."

Wondering if I should make him. Because that evening, under a star-sprinkled, perfect October sky, 675 people showed up for dinner. They just kept streaming in through the trees. I guess there were more people than we had imagined who needed a dinner with friends. We scrambled to set up another hundred feet of table, fired up a small generator for more lights, and kept passing the food down until everyone had more than enough.

It was a banquet of epic proportions. I think it was the kind of banquet Jesus was talking about when he said, "Tell everyone you meet to come to the banquet."[7]

IN JESUS' HILLSIDE sermon, as he described his kingdom, he said, "You have heard that it was said, 'Love your neighbor and hate your enemy.' But I tell you, love your enemies . . ."[8]

So the question lingers, who is my enemy? In this context, I see Jesus describing "your enemy" as anyone different from you in any way—anyone possessing a certain characteristic that makes it uncomfortable for you to accept and include them. It could be skin color, income, nationality, neighborhood, type of family.

We need to form a more biblical response to those we have made our enemies. We need to step back and honestly ask ourselves whether our positions and biases are biblical, or have we allowed culture or religious tradition to influence our judgment?

What will our response be to immigrants?

FOR SOME ODD reason certain Christians have adopted a political position against immigrants, as though it is biblical to despise them. People sneer at immigrants like the Jews did at the Samaritans. I hear people justify their views on certain kinds of people based on the legality of their immigration statuses. I wonder, does immigration status matter to God? The truth is, every person is wanted by God. And if every person is wanted by God, then they must be embraced by his followers. Not just tolerated, but welcomed, invited in, included, loved. If they have needs, we must meet them. The church must call its people to embrace the immigrant.

What will our response be to women?

MAYBE WOMEN HAVE found equality in other realms of society, but not so much in the church. I naively believed women had been liberated in the sixties. I was wrong. I recently listened as a leader emphatically pronounced that his church would never allow a female worship leader. Where do people come up with that kind of doctrine? Certainly not the Bible.

The church must address the role of women in leadership. We cannot keep women marginalized and domesticated. The *imago Dei* resides at the core of every one of God's beautifully created people, and that matters most.

What will our response be to the gay community?

WHEN JESUS WALKED the ground of first-century Israel, adultery was the scourge of the day. His response was blunt and simple: "Drop your stones." Stop all the judging and hating. Show more grace; live in peace.

And maybe those two words sum up all Jesus came to say—grace and peace.

We have a new scourge du jour these days: homosexuality. Church people panic when a gay person walks through the door. We say things like, "Hate the sin, and love the sinner." Sounds nice, but I don't really see people living that way.

So how will we respond? Will we welcome them or ask them to leave? Do we treat them differently from the unmarried couple that has moved in together—and they lead a small group?

Since we have no clear response, we have become known as a bigoted and prejudiced people. I am perplexed as to why we have made this one issue in Scripture the greatest measure of spirituality. It all seems quite disproportionate.

I wonder what would happen if we became more about grace and peace. What if we actually followed the command of Jesus to put down our stones and showed more love?

What will our response be to those of different races?

I ACTUALLY THOUGHT we were doing better in this area as well until the church in the Bible Belt voted to exclude interracial couples.

Ridiculous.

Fortunately, other churches are setting a far more biblical example. I love hearing about churches like Mosaic in Los Angeles and Wilcrest in Houston, where racial diversity is championed. Increasingly, churches are celebrating race. We must continue down this path to bring people of every race, background, and ethnicity together in meaningful ways: leading together, worshipping together . . . sitting around dining room tables together.

I am not only addressing suburban, white churches here. My challenge is to all churches. Too often our churches are dominated by a single ethnicity or race; it's time for all of us to embrace the other, particularly in our worship.

CARRIED TO THE TABLE

IT WAS THE first stop on our Hungry for Love Tour. I was waiting for Leeland to finish its set (before I was to take the stage to speak about *taking pieces of heaven to places of hell on earth*), when Leeland explained the message behind his song "Carried to the Table."

The song was inspired by the true story in 2 Samuel, when King David sent for Saul's last surviving relative, Mephibosheth. Mephibosheth was poor, broken, and had two lame legs.

Believing David had sent for him to punish him or extract revenge for his grandfather Saul's repeated attempts to end David's life, Mephibosheth arrived at the palace begging David for mercy, asking, "What do you want with a dog like me?"

David laughed. "No, I've invited you to come and be included at my palace."

From that day on, Mephibosheth always ate at the king's table.[9]

He used to be the poor one. He used to be the broken one. He used to be the lame one. Now, every day he was the one carried to the table of the king.

It's like that for you and me. The King of Kings invites you in, in spite of all that's messed up in your life.

You see, the King has sent for you. He waits for you to arrive. You think he's angry with you for all your mistakes. You think he wants you to pay a price, to suffer. You think you are too lame and dirty to come into his presence. But it's not like that. He wants to redeem you. The filth and the grime don't bother him . . . he's seen it before.

So come.

His table is set for you.

THE LONG DAY in Africa felt longer as I walked the dusty road back to my dingy guest house by the beach in Monrovia. When I stepped through the creaking screen door I found three young short-term volunteers around a table having dinner.

"You ate dinner already?" one of them asked, surprised that I was back so quickly.

"No, they said they had no food for me," I answered quietly.

"Have a seat and eat with us, Palmer," they offered warmly.

I offered a polite "No, it's okay," then quickly took them up on their offer.

The serving dishes were already empty, so they took food from each of their own plates until there was enough to fill mine.

Dinner that night tasted better than I could have imagined. In hindsight, maybe it wasn't the food that tasted so good, but the invitation to share a meal with friends.

CHAPTER 7

We Will Become Social Entrepreneurs and Empower Fair Trade

BOYD SHOWED UP AT MY brother's house on the edge of Lilongwe at dinnertime. He held his fragile infant daughter closely, but she still cried. She was hungry.

We'd known Boyd for years. His life had been plagued by pain. He walked with a limp, because his leg had rotted in the Lilongwe Central Hospital where he waited three days to see a doctor after a car shattered his femur. His wife had died in labor less than a month earlier, and now his infant daughter was obviously malnourished.

"Paul, my baby's hungry, and I have no money for the formula. Can you help me?"

"Sure, Boyd, get in the car, and we'll go pick some up." Paul's seven-year-old daughter, Bess, jumped in with them to ride along. When they stopped and bought the formula, it was far more expensive than Paul had imagined. Twenty-four dollars for one can. Boyd's entire monthly income would not equal the price of just one can of baby formula. Paul also picked up several one-liter bottles of purified water. Dysentery from the bad water in the village was more of a threat than starvation.

Paul and Bess drove Boyd back to his village and dropped him off with the baby. Bess was silent most of the drive home. Finally, she turned and asked, "Dad, how long will the formula feed baby Chisomo?"

"About a month, Bess, about a month," Paul answered softly.

She was quiet again for a moment, "How will she eat after that?"

"I don't know, Bess."

When they pulled up to their house, Bess ran out to find her seven-year-old cousin Charlotte. "You have to help me, Charlotte! There's a hungry baby named Chisomo, and we need to find some money to feed her."

Charlotte was in. The next day they walked through the fields near their house picking lilacs. Then they came back home and found a few pieces of cheesecloth in their mothers' closets and tied together dozens of small sacks filled with the blossoms. Next they went door-to-door selling their product to faculty and staff, telling them, "If you put this pouch in your dresser drawer, your clothes will smell like flowers in the morning."

Selling their scented pouches for a dollar each, they soon had enough money for formula and purified water for the next month, then the next. They continued selling lilac pouches and buying baby formula until Chisomo was big enough and strong enough to eat *nsima* and *chambo* (the ground maize and fish all Malawians love).

Two seven-year-old entrepreneurs rescued one infant from the grip of extreme poverty. Think what would happen if all of us heard the cry of hungry baby girls.

Bess and Charlotte are on to something spectacular, and it's good and beautiful and godly.

A NEW KIND OF ENTREPRENEUR

THE FIRST MAJOR I declared in college was business. There were at least half a dozen other business majors on our dorm floor my freshman year. We carried folded copies of the *Wall Street Journal* under our arms, wore suits and ties to seminars hosted by successful executives, bought cheap cigars to smoke in the hot tub as we talked about making millions, and as often as possible, we worked the word *entrepreneur* into a sentence.

Todd, who lived in the room next door, scrawled EN-TERPRENEUR in red marker on a piece of cardboard and taped it to his door. Gary taunted him relentlessly. "Todd, how in the world are you going to be an entrepreneur if you can't even spell the word?"

We liked the word because we were sure it was our ticket to making a million by thirty. Personally, I was tired of being the poor missionary kid whose parents didn't have enough money to buy a new ball when we popped the only one we owned on the thorny palm nut trees at the end of our soccer field in the jungle.

However, I didn't graduate a business major. I eventually realized there had to be more to life than hoping to make a pile of money. I stopped using the word *entrepreneur*—until recently, when I realized that an economic revolution for justice and compassion was sweeping the globe.

I knew of dozens of nonprofits printing T-shirts for a cause. What I didn't know was that a movement with greater substance was forming. A tsunami of change was breaking on the economic landscape. A new breed of entrepreneur was emerging. They had heart and soul. They were for the poor, for the environment, for the worker, for the blighted community, and for the marginalized widow.

There's a name for people like this, people with a heart and passion like Bess and Charlotte. They are called *social entrepreneurs*.

ECONOMIC REVOLUTION

WE LIVE AT a time when a generation is rewriting the world's economic structure.

It used to be that turning a profit was all that mattered. The mountain ranges of Zimbabwe were stripped for their ore, the virgin forest of Brazil was slashed for its timber, the automobile factories in Detroit pumped their chemical waste into the Rouge River, factory workers making running shoes in Bangladesh were cursed and abused when production slipped, and unscrupulous Wall Street brokers stole billions from the rich. All in the name of profit. All in the name of better economics.

That kind of profit-taking is dying. The old world of greed is crumbling, and a new way of profiting for all is emerging from the rubble.

Of all the epic shifts in culture, the move from egocentric business models to social entrepreneurship is probably the greatest. Humanity as a whole is bending toward justice and mercy and generosity.

Not just a few things are changing. *Everything* is changing. The history books are being written as we breathe. In much the same way that Ronald Reagan helped free the Eastern Bloc Communist workers, new value is being placed on the workers, their families, their communities. This is a "tectonic shift so profound that everything is transformed."[1]

Dedicated to unharnessing the potential of individuals and communities in developing nations to make a difference in the world through business, social entrepreneurs seek to help people live with greater dignity and realize they have the power to rise out of the poverty trap. Creative millennials are living this out every day as they find scalable solutions to the world's most vexing socioeconomic problems.

They are a tenacious breed. They innovate, adapt, and improvise. They are fearless in taking bold risks. They are change makers. They are the people and tribes coming together to share the load of changing the lives of others for good. They take an integrative approach, drawing on the best thinking and ideas from the business world, as well as the nonprofit community.

Social entrepreneurs bring change in business practices as well as change in the ways communities live. They bring awareness and suggestions for how to go from old, damaging ways of behavior—such as slash-and-burn farming—to new, life-sustaining, healthy ways. A critical power of social entrepreneurship is the way it inspires people in underdeveloped communities to create their own change.

The social entrepreneur's motivation is not personal gain. They see the world as a dynamically connected family where all people have a moral responsibility to serve the common good.

Their dream is to renew blighted neighborhoods, restore war-torn countries, and give dignity to the marginalized.

The Bible lays a strong foundation for a life and work dedicated to this kind of service. In Acts 9, Paul the Apostle writes about a Christ-follower in Joppa named Tabitha (her Greek name is Dorcas) and how she was famous for doing good and helping the poor. She was not only deeply loved by the people she served, she was prized by God. So much so that when she unexpectedly died, he brought her back to life.

In his letter to the Christians in Corinth, Paul writes,

"Now to each one the manifestation of the Spirit is given for the common good."[2] This concept of being for the common good is a striking idea. It grinds just a bit against the grain of Western individualism that has been adopted by the church. This view is reflected even in our language, with such terms as "my personal savior."

The truth is God created us to care for each other. This is what the first church was all about: "All the believers were together and had everything in common."[3]

God's people today must rediscover the value of work, business, and enterprise being for the good of others, as well as for oneself. It's time for us to break free of our individualistic, self-profiting culture and create a new model.

SADLY, THE INTERNATIONAL aid community of the last half century has been grossly inefficient and is one of those old models that must change. Growing up in Africa I knew the aid community well. I went to school with their children. They were the ones chauffeured to school in imported Suburbans. I've been in their ice-cold, multistoried homes, behind gated walls in the most affluent neighborhoods. Their parents received "hardship pay."

Too much aid money from affluent nations has been spent housing and protecting its workers in developing countries, where only infinitesimal amounts of donor aid have finally trickled down to meet actual community needs.

The 1980s and '90s saw the growth of massive nonprofits and NGOs (nongovernmental organizations). Again, the overhead was staggering. Excessive amounts were spent on television advertisements about starvation and extreme poverty. Money flowed in, but the NGOs and nonprofits grew empires, not communities. They hired Wall Street executives to watch the bottom line, built mansions on the ground to house their staff, and purchased absurd numbers of SUVs. They overpaid staff, creating a false economy. They siphoned so much for "operations" that again, only pennies on the dollar ended up directed toward real change in desperate communities.

The millennial social entrepreneurs are, on the other hand, austere and efficient. Their operational machine is not perfect. They make lots of mistakes. They are naively ambitious. They sometimes trust the wrong people and get burned . . . but they run economically soulful operations that are effective.

And their economics are working. They are having an impact. They are growing viable economies in destitute communities. They are turning garbage-dump pickers into shop owners, brothel prostitutes into seamstresses, and refugees into jewelry artisans.

The underlying ethos of social entrepreneurship is possibly the most important aspect of the movement: to guide inherently unjust and inequitable societies to a new equilibrium that is fair and good for all.[4]

Social entrepreneurs initiate, collaborate, take risks, and can change course quickly. They fearlessly tackle problems that appear daunting. They refuse adages such as "It can't be done." Or the idea that issues like malaria are "too great for solving." They may lack the expertise, but they believe somewhere along the way God will lead them to the right person, provide just enough resources, open the closed door. They watch and learn. They try—fail—and try again. They are relentless in their determination to turn the tide.

Bill Drayton, founder of Ashoka (a global nonprofit dedicated to identifying and investing in social entrepreneurs), describes the passion of social entrepreneurs like this:

> The job of the social entrepreneur is to recognize when a part of society is not working and to solve the problem by changing the system; spreading solutions, and persuading an entire society to take new leaps. Social entrepreneurs are not content just to give a fish or to teach how to fish. They will not rest until they have revolutionized the fishing industry.[5]

There's something contagious about social entrepreneurship. These change makers have a way of attracting and multiplying and reproducing more change makers. They collaborate like tribes and grow stronger.

Traditional business models by nature cause isolation. They create idea vacuums to protect their best thinking. They lock their most creative people and best ideas behind bolted doors and security cameras.

Social entrepreneurs, on the other hand, are open-platform thinkers.

They know our best ideas proliferate when they are shared. Collective purpose is what makes social entrepreneurs so powerful. When we collaborate and work as one, our strength compounds exponentially.

Take Tyler Merrick, for example. He labels himself a social capitalist. I love it.

Tyler is part of a movement to build a new kind of capitalism.

For centuries, Western capitalism has been for the good of self, the good of me. Generation justice, however, is changing the way we think about turning a profit.

Merrick says early in his business life it hit him. "If we're going to build a brand, why don't we do it with something that has another level of depth?"[6] He is turning a new kind of profit—one that profits hurting people in broken places.

Out of Merrick's passion, Project 7 was born: a business dedicated to making *Products for Good*. They manufacture products we use every day—like bottled water, gum, mints, and coffee—in countries with need. Project 7's profit is then used to give back to those countries in seven areas of need: Feed the Hungry, Heal the Sick, Hope for Peace, House the Homeless, Quench the Thirsty, Teach them Well, and Save the Earth. All of this is inspired by Jesus' words in Matthew 25.

Merrick's kind of capitalism is profiting everyone.

I write all this to say the wave is cresting—dive in. We need more social entrepreneurs like Tyler Merrick. We need greater collaboration among social entrepreneurs. Everyone can participate. You can participate. Our hope for the Barefoot Tribe is to create a global network of collaborative entrepreneurship that will pool their best thinking, give their best effort, and share their most valuable resources to finally tip the scales toward justice and dignity.

TRADE FAIR

THE ARTIFACT VENDORS stopped by our home in Liberia often, especially when they knew we had guests from America. They all billed themselves as "Cheap-Cheap Charlie." They sold things like carved mahogany elephants, ebony candlestick holders, and tie-dye tablecloths.

I learned early on that everything was negotiable. As a twelve-year-old I prided myself in being able to beat the Charlies down to whatever price our guest wanted to pay, usually well below half of the original asking price.

The Charlies had a knack for stopping by at dinnertime, like good vacuum cleaner salesmen. What they didn't know I knew about them was that they were hungry. I knew they had spent their day walking door-to-door in the blazing African heat. Now the sun was setting. We, the expatriates, were their last hope for food for their family.

I would start with a ridiculously low price. They would say, "I paid more than that to the carver." But I was relentless. I spoke Liberian English like a native, so I would banter and barter and point out flaws in their wares. Because I knew they would cave. I knew they were hungry.

I've since stopped doing that.

The first time I saw a man sitting on the side of the road in Africa using a carpenter's hammer to break boulders into one-inch granite pieces for concrete mix, I had a hard time believing what I was seeing. He was a proud father in front of his mud hut with a thatched roof and with two small boys looking over his shoulder, breaking rocks with a hammer—trying to build a pile large enough for the trucks from the city to stop and buy a load. How long would that take? A month? How much would they pay him? Hardly anything. He had to compete with the corporate granite crushers in the quarries that used large machines to crush rock by the ton.

So he takes whatever he is offered.

It's not enough to live on.

It's not enough to feed his two sons.

Maybe this gnawed at me the most. A man—made in the image of God—sitting in the dirt, breaking rocks with a hammer.

I was certain this man was an anomaly. Last spring, however, as we drove down the mountain called Beautiful (just behind Port-au-Prince), we rounded a bend to see a man sitting on the ground, breaking rocks with a hammer.

A mile down the road I asked our driver to pull over where a row of Haitian vendors sell their carvings and artifacts to tourists. The sun was setting, and I could see that some of the vendors were closing the doors to their small shops. I waved from the window that we were coming. I knew they would be glad to see a van full of "Blancs." As we climbed out of the van, I told my buddy Jay, "This is a great place to pick up machetes for our sons!" But before I was even out of the van, I saw a vendor jogging our way with two machetes in his hand. I stepped out, laughing, "How in the world did you know we wanted machetes?"

"*Mon amie,* you were here last year, and you bought four machetes!" (Yes, I needed four. I have four sons.)

Who knew my reputation would precede me? And who knew this vendor would remember me from a year ago?

"Okay, these are perfect. How much are you asking?"

"Just pay me what you paid last year," he answered confidently. "Fifteen dollars each."

I was quite certain I had beat him down to five dollars each, but now I couldn't get the man breaking rocks with a hammer out of my mind.

"Sure." I smiled and said, "I'll pay the fifteen dollars each."

Just because we can, doesn't mean we should.

———

I THINK GENERATIONS past did not mind raping the land and the poor to turn a profit. That's why bulldozers are clearing the Amazon rain forest for soy plantations, to grow fuel for cars in L.A. That's why West African countries are cutting down one-hundred-year-old virgin jungles to sell mahogany to furniture makers in Atlanta. And that's why tire companies coerce Brazilian rubber growers into making children climb their trees to pick more rubber.

Not this generation, though. They don't mind profiting less in order for the poor of Guatemala, or Bolivia, or Côte d'Ivoire to earn more. They demand that trade be fair.

Fair trade is a biblical value. The wise king Solomon said, "A poor person's farm may produce much food, but injustice sweeps it all away."[7] The ancient prophet Isaiah spoke for God and said, "Stop exploiting your workers."[8] God cannot bless you when you live like that.

But we are a consumer culture and we like our cheap junk, so we tend to not ask questions about why a dress shirt at Ross only costs $4.99. We want lots of stuff, and we want it for the price of a cheeseburger.

Just because we can pay the cotton growers of Mali (who in their desperation will accept what is offered), or the textile artisans of India, or the banana farmers of Peru less—less than they can live on—does not mean we should.

I've stopped haggling with vendors.

Maybe all of us need to shop and buy more conscientiously, more intelligently, more biblically.

What's a few dollars to you and me—loose change? For a man in Haiti it means food and shelter and an education for his children.

ECO-CONSCIENCE

AT THE GROVE we've partnered with a community of farmers in Guatemala to grow The Grove's coffee because fair trade empowers the poor.

This was our millennial coffee shop manager's idea. So he flew to Guatemala and drove eight hours deep into the jungle mountains to meet the co-op of farmers who grow coffee; to ensure we pay them a fair price, enough for them to feed their families and for their children to attend school.

How you buy and what you buy matters. That's the idea of fair trade. "Fair trade is deliberately biased towards the inclusion of marginalized producers. . . . It seeks to level the playing field for those without a voice or access to multiple markets."[9] So buy with a conscience.

The spending habits of affluent people in wealthy nations directly affect the poor in impoverished nations. When we make a habit of buying from businesses that exploit a desperate workforce, like the Ivorians who grow cocoa for multinational chocolate corporations, we feed the problem.

In Côte d'Ivoire, the source of practically 40 percent of the world's chocolate, about 109,000 children are illegally used in the harvest of cocoa. Some would go so far as to call it slave labor, because they earn practically nothing from their work. The chocolate conglomerates know this, but turn a blind eye. "There's a dirty secret in the chocolate business, and once people find out about it, their chocolate doesn't taste as sweet anymore."[10]

This kind of abuse and exploitation is rampant in Africa, Asia, and Latin America. For example, almost 60 percent of Ethiopian children are forced to work in order for their families to survive. They earn about a dollar a month, usually working as domestic servants, or in gritty gold mines, or as farmhands.

In Zimbabwe, under the brutal dictatorial rule of Africa's madman Robert Mugabe, children have been exploited in the worst ways. In his economic desperation, Mugabe made popular a program he dubbed Learn as You Earn, a ploy to pull children out of school and force them to work for practically nothing on government-owned farms and in diamond mines.

In Pakistan, children are regularly abducted, rented, bought, and sold like property. The Punjab province is most notorious for its abuse of child workers, who stitch rugs, craft musical instruments, and make soccer balls for sporting-goods companies in places like Beverton.[11]

In the United States, we keep feeding the big-box retailers, because we can get toilet paper for a buck. We turn a blind eye to what it takes for them to offer us our junk so cheap. We like the prices, so we don't ask the important questions: Who has been exploited? Who have they put out of business? What land have they pillaged?

We've sold our souls for the coupon section in the daily paper.

I challenge you to do your homework on the businesses and companies you patronize.

When we are careless or care less about what we buy, we keep the poor poor. When we buy with a conscience and become educated in our spending, we help narrow the gap between the affluent and the needy. This is a large part of what global economist Jeffrey Sachs says must happen for us to realistically end extreme poverty.

When I lived in Malawi, the government's minimum wage was set at thirty-five kwachas a day. That was about fifty cents.

Here's what chafed me. Expatriates who employed a

Malawian workforce often paid only that amount. It was exploitation at its worst. No one anywhere can feed their family on fifty cents a day. Yet tobacco growers boast about how much money they make, because they get away with paying their workers a shamefully low wage.

God will judge that.

Jesus' brother James warns,

Your money is corrupt and your fine clothes stink. Your greedy luxuries are a cancer in your gut, destroying your life from within. You thought you were piling up wealth. What you've piled up is judgment. All the workers you've exploited and cheated cry out for judgment. The groans of the workers you used and abused are a roar in the ears of the Master Avenger. You've looted the earth and lived it up.[12]

The Bible is clear that we have a responsibility to the poor to empower them to earn a living, not to exploit them in their desperation.

Fair trade is a way to demand justice for the marginalized.

The tribal vision is for the church of the future to lead the global efforts for sustainable development and to help create a world where equity—not greed—is a core value of all trade and commerce. This is part of the "good news for the poor and freedom for the oppressed" that Jesus said he came to bring.[13] If this was important to the Christ, it must be important to you. Because it's the poorest of the poor who suffer most in the world of unfair trade.

THE COMPASSION NERVE

A FASCINATING RECENT discovery in neuroscience tells us that God has actually hardwired every human being for compassion, to look to interests outside of our own. Deep inside every person is the vagus nerve, from the Latin *vagus* for "wandering." It's appropriately named, since the nerve starts at the top of the spinal cord and winds through the body's core, affecting practically every major organ—even affecting our breathing and heart rate.

When something moves us emotionally—such as beauty or generosity or our favorite song performed live—the vagus nerve fires and sends signals throughout the body, and we feel something: love, joy, happiness, empathy, compassion. That's why many have begun to call this the "Compassion Nerve."[14]

Some have argued that of all the human instincts, compassion is the strongest. Studies have shown that the most empathetic people, the ones who demonstrate the greatest sympathy and empathy for others, become the ones who thrive and flourish more.[15]

What has amazed neuroscientists most is that it's not only our own experiences that activate the vagus nerve, but the nerve reacts to what is happening in the lives of other people near us. If a friend begins to cry, the vagus nerve fires. When you hear an inspiring story, the vagus nerve reacts. When your bride walks down the aisle, when your son graduates, when your best friend loses her mother, when you hold an orphaned child in Haiti . . . That connection to others, that compassion, moves you deep on the inside.

God made us for compassion. God created our inmost beings to care deeply for others.

It is in the very fabric of our makeup to follow the path of social entrepreneurship and fair trade.

That's why the tribe comes alive when they see a broken system, such as children being forced to harvest cocoa in Côte d'Ivoire. They are burdened with that God-given compassion. That powerful emotion connects with their internal passions and abilities. When those forces come together, they begin to seek innovative ways to create a new system.

It's time for you and me to join them, to demand and create something that benefits more than just ourselves, that protects artisans from exploitation, while empowering them to rise out of the mire of poverty. It's time to demand a new way of doing business for Western Christians, a new way of being responsible consumers who don't perpetuate unfair trade. A way that is good and profitable for everyone.

CHAPTER 8
We Will Become Modern-Day Abolitionists

WHEN MY FRIEND PAT McCULLAH tells people why he's given his life to rescuing sexually exploited girls, he tells them about fifteen-year-old "Debbie." One evening a friend from Debbie's school, Bianca, called to say she was stopping by to say hi. Debbie met her in the driveway in her pajamas. Bianca had two men with her Debbie had never met; the one driving the large Cadillac called himself Primetime.

When she gave Bianca a hug good-bye, Primetime grabbed her from behind and pushed her into the car, where her mouth and hands were duct-taped together. They drove her to a filthy apartment filled with young men who raped her for hours.

For the next month she was caged in a dog kennel under a bed, only let out to be sold to middle-aged men for sex. Her captors advertised her on Craigslist. She says at least fifty men responded to the ad. Finally, another girl, Miya, escaped the apartment and told the police about Debbie.

They searched the apartment but didn't find her. Still suspicious a few days later, they broke down the doors to the same apartment. Debbie said she heard Officer James Perry calling her name but was too frightened to answer.

"I didn't know what to say; I was just lying in the cage under the bed, stiff as a board, shaking."

When Officer Perry opened the cage door the only words he could utter were, "Oh, my God!"

Oh, my God is right. Oh, my God, why are we allowing these kinds of things to happen among us? This is not some faraway place like Phuket. This is Phoenix. This is happening in the city I live in!

SLAVES IN THE SUBURBS

WE ALL KNOW about the sexual exploitation of girls and young women in places like Manila and Mombasa, but we don't think much about the exploitation of girls in places like Portland and Phoenix. This generation, though, knows about it and wants it stopped.

This tribe is incensed by slavery. They are angry about

what is happening to girls like Debbie in places like Phoenix. They have declared themselves "modern-day abolitionists."

Here are the numbers and the facts: an estimated twenty-seven million people are held in slavery worldwide. This means there are more slaves in the world today than were taken from Africa during three hundred years of trans-atlantic slave trade. We now have more slaves among us than at any other time in human history.

After drug trafficking, human trafficking is tied with the illegal arms trade as the second largest criminal industry in the world, and it is the fastest growing. In the United States alone, it is estimated there are two hundred thousand slaves. More than half of the victims are believed to be children—worldwide an estimated 1.2 million children are trafficked each year. The FBI says the average age of a new prostitute in the United States is thirteen.

Why don't we hear more? Why don't we say more? Why are we not doing more?

Minors are the preferred mark for traffickers. They say they are easy targets. Former FBI assistant director Chip Burrus says, "These predators are particularly adept at read-ing kids and knowing what their vulnerabilities are. . . . What you see, time and time again, is that the predators will adapt their means to whatever the young people are doing—whether it's malls, whether it's ski slopes, whether it's beaches."[1]

I recently had a conversation with Anny Donewald, founder of Eve's Angels.

Living in Chicago, just out of college, and in her early

twenties, Anny was sucked into prostitution. She said her life spiraled for years.

Today, Anny is an advocate for all the young women who have been deceived and misled and forced to sell their bodies. Anny has completely dedicated her life to following God, who has become her *father*—instead of the pimp who controlled her life for so many years.

The prostitution business is epidemic. Eighty-seven million women a day are sold for sex around the world. But Anny says the larger epidemic is *ignorance*.

What we need, she insists, is a revolution to change our perception of the problem. Anny refuses to use the words *human trafficking*. She says that's just a nice way for church people to talk about a filthy problem. She wants pimps to be called pimps, and pimping, pimping. She swore a few times as we talked, because she can no longer contain the frustration of watching so many Christians remain ambivalent to the pimps and prostitution in our country.

The myth, Anny explained, is that women are imported from places like Central America. The real sex trade, however, is happening domestically. We have our own system that needs to be exposed. She is demanding that more pimps be prosecuted and given harsher sentences. She is promoting a national campaign for men to take a pledge to stop frequenting the strip clubs and massage parlors where the bodies of the young women of our county are being sold.

I'm with her. It's time for a revolution.

BREAK THE CHAINS

JESUS' WORDS WERE strangely prophetic when he said he had come to free the captives. How did he know that two thousand years later, we would still have the captives among us, silenced and suffering? When he talks about his mission here on earth, he quotes the ancient prophet Isaiah, who wrote, "This is the kind of fast day I'm after: to break the chains of injustice, get rid of exploitation in the workplace, free the oppressed."[2]

People who will give their lives to liberation are the kind of people Jesus was after. How do we miss this clear call to live the gospel? Isaiah doesn't mince words. The church for the most part has simply chosen to ignore them. Read the passage again. He says God could care less about religious pageantry, church polity, and pious tradition. He's not so interested in our Greek verb conjugations and Hebrew root words. What he wants is a church that will do something about the desperate people all around us. Give them dignity, freedom, respect, a way to earn a living. When we live like that, Isaiah says, *then* God will hear your prayer. Then he will be pleased with your spirituality.

Why has the evangelical church of the past hundred years cut these pages out of its Holy Bible?

God and the Bible have always been about liberation.

The Bible beats with God's passion for justice and freedom. Oppression disturbs the heart of God. The cry for freedom originates with God himself: "Let my people go!"[3] He is the God of liberation. He freed the Jewish people from Babylon, he freed Joseph from the pit, he freed Mordecai from the gallows, he freed Paul from a Roman prison, he freed ten vagrants from leprosy, he freed Christ from the tomb. He frees you and me for eternity. And he wants you (and me and everyone who follows him) to free the exploited women and children everywhere.

Giving liberty to others is not only our moral duty; it makes the name of God famous. That's what God told Moses when he freed the people in Egypt. "[And] when I raise my powerful hand and bring out the Israelites, the Egyptians will know that I am the LORD."[4] "[I will] show you my power" and "spread my fame throughout the earth."[5]

THE ABOLITIONISTS

A TRIBE HAS formed of modern-day abolitionists. They take the words of Isaiah and Jesus seriously. David Batstone is one of them. When David, a Westmont College grad, realized the servers in his favorite Bay Area Indian restaurant were child slaves, he took a year off of work to track the traffickers.

Batstone flew to Chiang Mai, Thailand, where he was introduced to Kru Nam. Kru was a painter who each day on the walk to her studio passed a dozen or more children—ten-, eleven-, twelve-year-olds—sleeping on the edge of the canal. One morning, she carried canvases and brushes with her and asked the kids to paint their stories. Their art was disturbing. They painted graphic images of kidnapping and sexual abuse.

As she asked them to share more, she learned they were not Thai. They were from Myanmar, Laos, Cambodia, and China. Some were sold by parents because of poverty, some were kidnapped, some were promised school. They were all sex slaves. Once in Thailand they were taken to karaoke bars where sex tourists paid to abuse them.

They told Kru, "We are the lucky ones."

"Lucky?" she blurted out. "How?"

"We have escaped," they explained. "Our friends are still trapped in the karaoke bars."

Kru was furious. That night she marched into a karaoke bar where she found two small girls talking to men. She grabbed them and ran. The next night she hit another karaoke bar. When David met Kru, her rescue count was at twenty-seven, but she was in hiding because the karaoke bar owners of Chiang Mai wanted her dead. That's when Dave committed to raising funds to build a refuge for the eighty-eight kids Kru had rescued, and the count is growing.

———

MARK SOUTH IS another modern-day abolitionist. Mark is a Biola University grad who pastors a church and runs a coffee shop near Sacramento. Mark doesn't pay his employees a cent. This is because they don't call themselves baristas at Origin Coffee & Tea. Mark says they are abolitionists. Over a hundred of them volunteer in order for profits (more than twenty thousand dollars in their first year of operation) from the coffee shop to go toward rescuing girls from slavery. Mark says his abolitionists are storytellers who educate their customers about the growing sex-trade industry in Nor Cal and challenge them to take action in their community, as well as in places such as Chiang Mai.[6]

———————

MATT WAS FRESH off the plane from Thailand when he sat in my office and told me with calm determination about the sting he had just taken part in with the Thai police. They arrested eight brothel madams, karaoke bar managers, and massage parlor owners. They freed forty-four girls and young women and shut down more than a dozen child prostitution rings. The youngest girls, he said, were locked behind metal doors.

He told me about "Ning," a fifteen-year-old sold by her own mother to a brothel where she was held prisoner. It took just two days to sell her virginity for six hundred dollars. When Matt went undercover into her brothel, filming with a hidden camera, she handed him a crumpled dollar bill with the urgent message scribbled in Thai, "Please rescue me!"

He did.

Matt leads an organization, Exodus Road, committed to walking into the filthy business of child prostitution to end it. He and his team go into the bars and brothels with hidden cameras to gather surveillance. They find underage girls and quietly tell them they have come to set them free. The kingpins hate them. They want them dead. They send them bullets in the mail when their covers are blown. Matt says he risks his life because, "I have three young daughters. If my eight-year-old daughter was being sold for sex, I would hope with all of my heart that someone like me would go in and rescue someone like her."

Matt is not waiting for someone else or some government agency to go into the places of hell on earth.

Matt said he loved having coffee with one of our church leaders named John, because after hearing his story, John said, "If not the church, then who?"

If not now, then when?

Before Matt left my office he calmly looked me in the eye and said, "Will you help me?"

I smiled and answered confidently, "Sure, we will. I can think of at least a dozen police officers and former Marines here at our church that would be willing to go and help you."

"No, Palmer, I mean you! Will you come and help me?"

The smile faded from my face.

"Yes, Matt, I will. I must." And I have.

If not me, then who?

————————

I INVITE YOU to join this tribe of abolitionists. Here are a few simple suggestions:

1. Tell your sons and daughters.

IN THE SAME way we warn our children about the devil in hell, warn them about the devil in their shopping malls and outside their school fences.

2. *Speak out against the establishments in your community that promote lasciviousness.*

YOU KNOW WHERE the places in your community are that attract the worst kind of humanity, like flies to dung. Demand they close their doors.

3. *Join the abolitionists.*

RAISE AWARENESS OF the problem everywhere. Blog, post on Facebook, write articles. We are a nation strangely silent about our sin. We will have to be honest and open about the problem and pour our passions and resources into making it stop.

CHAPTER 9
We Will End
Extreme Poverty

NOT LONG AFTER I FINISHED grad school the head basketball coach from my university mentioned that other coaches in our conference were recruiting ringers from Africa. Since that was my home, he asked if I had any leads. I did. I knew two brothers who were great ballers, living as refugees in Côte d'Ivoire after fleeing the Liberian war.

I had been planning a trip to Côte d'Ivoire to encourage students from African Bible College, where I taught before the civil war broke out, who were living as refugees. So I invited Coach to join me.

We flew fourteen hours to Abidjan loaded with five suitcases filled with shoes, jeans, and shirts for my dozens of Liberian friends living in exile in Danané. We landed at 2:00 a.m. The brothers, Jay and Morris, met us at the airport, wide-awake and smiling ear to ear. Jay was six-six. I had coached against him for several years in Yekepa before the war and knew he was a beast on the court. I thought he should have no problem playing college ball in the U.S. His younger brother, Morris, was a six-foot, lightning-quick guard with mad handles, and he could even dunk!

The next day Coach had them shoot around, and he later watched Morris in a first-division game. He was impressed. That evening, we drove the brothers back to their house in the gritty slums of Treichville. Jay, friendly as always, offered, "Coach, Palmer, do you want to see our home?"

I parked the jeep, and we followed Jay down mucky dirt paths that wound between the shacks. Finally we reached the unfinished shell of a concrete block house, with a tin roof and boarded-up windows. We walked into a bare concrete room with five thin foam mattresses on the ground. Each was meticulously made with a small, tattered blanket folded at the foot. Five pairs of shoes neatly lined the wall to my right. There was no furniture, not even a chair. Beaming with pride, Jay smiled, "This is our home. Morris and I, with our three other brothers, rent this one room."

The three younger brothers were all in school. Jay and Morris, who had both graduated from high school just before the war, worked odd jobs to earn enough to feed the five brothers living in exile. Their parents had been left behind in Liberia, trapped behind rebel lines.

"How much does it cost a day to feed the five of you?" I asked.

"Only a hundred CFA a day each, Palmer."

"Jay, you're living on one hundred CFA a day?!"

"Sure," Jay answered. "With a hundred CFA I can buy a cup of rice and small palm oil to put on top."

At the time, one hundred CFA equaled a quarter. The five brothers were scratching out an existence on twenty-five cents a day.

Coach had only one scholarship available, so when he took Morris to America, Jay was left behind to help his three younger brothers survive on a dollar a day.

Until that moment years ago, I didn't know people could actually live on so little. But that's how a billion people around the world survive every day right now, one-sixth of our population.

It's tragic and it's a travesty . . . and we can end it.

———————

I REALIZE IT sounds audacious, but we really can end extreme poverty, and it's time.

The most respected experts in the field, like the economist Jeffrey Sachs, are convinced we can turn the tables on extreme poverty. Sachs believes it can be accomplished by the year 2025.[1] The key, however, is for all of us to commit to turning the tide. Our efforts must be collaborative, and massive, and concentrated. Then the poorest of the poor can be freed from the poverty trap.

It is time for us to care more about poverty. We've shrugged our shoulders long enough. We've turned a blind eye too many times. Now that the cry of the chronically hungry has reached your ears, what will you do?

The problem is we're simply not bothered enough by extreme poverty, let alone angered. We act saddened, but we certainly don't live like we should, or can, end it. We know the Bible says God is for the poor, but that never seems to motivate us to do much about their plight.

The evangelical has always been good at evangelism. But what people around us often don't know is that Jesus came to bring a better life now; in addition to eternal life, he came to tell us that *the kingdom of heaven has come to earth*. Please don't dismiss this as some cheap prosperity gospel. What I want you to see is that Jesus cared as much about poverty in the slums as he did about the poverty of the soul.

Jesus said, "Feed the hungry, give water to the thirsty, put clothes on the naked."[2] "If someone asks for your jacket, give them your shirt too."[3] "When the man outside your gate begs for food, and you ignore him, you will be the one who ends up in hell."[4]

When the five thousand were hungry, he stopped his preaching to give them something to eat. When the lame man lay useless on his mat, Jesus took him by the hand and made his legs strong again. When the lepers begged for mercy, he healed their sores.

Yes, the good news is spiritual and has eternal consequences for your soul, but the good news is also physical and must change the way you live every day.

At one point in Jesus' ministry he has the most revealing conversation with a successful businessman. The affluent young man approaches Jesus and asks what is required to gain a deeper spirituality. Jesus comes back with this: "Sell everything you have and give to the poor, and you will have treasure in heaven. Then come, follow me."[5] The man refuses. Jesus' summary is this: it's hard to get into heaven if you don't care about hell on earth.

CORRUPTION

WE OFTEN BLAME poverty in underdeveloped countries on the corruption of local and government officials. But here's the real corruption: the rampant waste by NGOs and Western government aid. Economics professor and author William Easterly says it well:

> People just assume if the money is budgeted for helping the poor that it goes to help the poor. . . . If you're just the average taxpayer in the U.S. or in Europe, there's not much incentive to investigate whether some poor village off in Ghana, West Africa, received the money or not. You can't mount your own investigation to find out. The press, unfortunately, doesn't seem to have enough motivation to really dig deep into whether the money reaches the poor, because they are mainly providing stories for U.S. consumption that are mainly mostly about

disasters striking Africa, wars and earthquake, and famines and droughts, and not about the more kind of pedestrian matter of, you know, did a dollar of aid money get to a baby in time to give them a re-hydration treatment so they wouldn't die from de-hydration?[6]

Many nonprofits don't do much better. One of our best-known Christian organizations flies its people around Africa in private jets and helicopters like they are aristocrats or ce-lebrities. A few weeks ago, my brother asked their helicopter pilot if my mother could hitch a ride back to the capital city to spare her the grueling eight-hour muddy, jarring, dusty drive through the Liberian jungle. The pilot said, "Sorry, members only."

There's too much overhead, too many layers of manage-ment, too much bureaucracy. When the money you give does not reach the people you care about, the people who need it the most, that's the real corruption.

Tribal people, however, are cutting out the middleman.

I SAY IT'S time to end extreme poverty, because all of us in the West—the developed world—have enjoyed two and a half centuries of economic prosperity. We are financially stable—actually, for the most part, we live in economic ex-cess. Now it's time to share what we have.

The cost is not too much anymore. It's doable. Here

are five critical steps all members of the tribe must consider:[7]

1. Make a personal commitment to end extreme poverty.

WE NEED YOU, your life, your influence. Maybe it begins with identifying just one community whose plight you can turn . . . or one infant who needs baby formula.

2. Become a voice for the extreme poor.

YOU DO NOT have to be rich or famous to be heard. Not anymore. Not in this new economy of social media and electronic access. The poor live in the silence of their desperation. They need a town crier. That voice is yours.

3. Champion sustainable development.

DONATIONS AND HANDOUTS are necessary and good, but they are not long-term solutions for the world's poor. Only when the most poor can grow their own food and find means to take some to market, allowing them to keep their children in school, will we tip the scales.

4. Promote investments in health, education, and infrastructure.

IN THE NEXT chapter we will look at the devastating effects of disease on a society. The simple addition of rural medical clinics is the first step in turning the tide. Accessible education is also at the root of empowering the next generation to break out of their poverty trap. Then infrastructure—something as simple as a road—gives rural farmers and artisans the access to markets that will turn the futures of entire villages, communities, and regions.

5. *Go and be with the poor.*

AT SOME POINT we need boots on the ground. At some point all the blogging, all the Facebooking, all the speeches begin to ring hollow. Someone must go and make sure the well is dug, the seeds are planted, the clinics are built. That someone could be you. That is why I keep saying, the tribe needs you—and you need the tribe.

THE CRY OF THE POOR

OUR RESPONSE TO the cry of the desperately poor may not always look the same. Sometimes they need relief, sometimes they need rehabilitation, and sometimes they most need development. Steve Corbett and Brian Fikkert write, "The failure to distinguish among these situations is one of the most common reasons that poverty-alleviation efforts often do [more harm than good.]"[8]

Relief

RELIEF IS OUR response to natural disasters, such as drought or a tsunami, or man-made crises like civil war and humanitarian abuses—like what the deranged rebel leader Joseph Kony has done to northern Uganda or the carnage and rape by M23 rebels that has wracked the Congo (DRC).

When an earthquake crumbles a city like Port-au-Prince, immediate relief is critical, not the kind of waiting and assessing that so many did after Haiti fell. That's why the tribe at The Grove responded just days after the earthquake by sending doctors, nurses, tents, and a truck filled with food for an orphanage.

Rehabilitation

WHEN THE IMMEDIATE crisis has passed, communities and regions most need help in restoring their towns, cities, school systems, and hospitals. They are always ready, often eager, to cooperate with responders to make this happen.

This is what our tribe is doing in Liberia after nineteen years of civil war devastated the country. We are primarily helping to get children and college students back into school, so they can flourish and pour back into their community. In the bush, we've named our effort "Mat to Mattress." Our goal is to help get the girls in the village, who sleep on bamboo mats on the dirt floor (many of whom will likely be forced to marry by the age of thirteen if they remain in the village), into schools where they will sleep in beds at night with mattresses and gain an education that will give them hope and a future.

Development

DEVELOPMENT IS THE long-term commitment to grow with a community and empower them to find sustainable solutions to their economic challenges.

In Malawi we have developed a church-to-community relationship with Chimpampha, a collection of villages outside Lilongwe. Our efforts there have included clean water projects, malaria prevention, and now a community clinic that the people from the villages will build and staff.

BEING WITH VS. DOING FOR

ESTHER HAVENS IS young, brilliant, and a gifted photographer. She travels the world with companies like Toms Shoes and documents their work. She describes herself as a humanitarian photographer. Esther has dedicated her pictures and passion to changing circumstances for the poor. She shares stunning images of hope to promote the work of organizations like buildOn, Malaria No More, and The Adventure Project.

Esther is making it her mission to change the way Americans act among the poor. She talks about how so often we go to places of affliction and poverty and take pictures from a distance. We treat the poor as objects, and we become a kind of disaster tourist.

Esther now teaches people how to be with the poor. How to sit with them in their places of desperation, hear their stories, feel their lives, and know them.

You see, our goal in ending poverty is not something to be done as outsiders, but something to be done *with* the poor. Our aim must be to fully engage them in a process that is participatory, a process that allows them to first decide whether or not they want the kind of help we offer. So our first task, then, is to empower them as decision makers. By allowing them to make their own decisions, their future is always in their hands, not the hands of others.

Most important is for deep, meaningful relationships to grow between the helpers and the helped. Recently, our tribal people have begun to take their children to Chimpampha. Beautiful, family-to-family relationships are being formed. This relational aspect of development, rehabilitation, or even relief is possibly the most critical aspect of our response to the poor. Sometimes we get lost in the task of drilling a well or building a dorm and miss the souls of the people we have come to care for.

Here's what happens when you live like this: you, the helper, grow. We sometimes think all of our work and passion is only for the good of the helped. We can miss the fact that the helper grows, too. I'm convinced there is a kind of spiritual transformation that only comes when we go to the most broken places and walk with the most desperate people. When we live like that we experience a spiritual growth that we will never find sitting in a cushioned pew on Sunday morning.

In my opinion, one of the church's great problems is that our sanctuaries fill on Sundays with spiritually stagnant people. They have sat in the same row, sung the same songs, attended the same small group, and prayed the same prayers for years. Long, long ago they stopped maturing spiritually. I am completely convinced there is a kind of spirituality that grows and flourishes only when we go to the places of hell on earth, only when we begin to live the gospel, only when we go into the homes of the broken—and our souls are disturbed and our hearts are broken. *Then* we grow. Then we flourish spiritually.

That's why I keep saying, *give your life away to change this world and God will change you.*

IT'S DOABLE

THE STATEMENT "WE can end extreme poverty" is not some naive, utopian fantasy. It is well within our reach.

As mentioned earlier, the World Bank estimates that approximately one-sixth of the world's population lives in extreme poverty today. Two generations ago that number was at one-half.[9] We've already come a long way.

Another thing to remember is that the goal is to end extreme poverty (those surviving on less than a dollar a day), not to make poor countries into wealthy nations. We are seeking to improve living standards in specific and practical ways, such as roads, power, water, and disease control. When you look at the task in this light, it is much less daunting than most make it out to be.

Changing circumstances in the most impoverished places requires only a fraction of what the wealthy of the world have. If nations will share more, if churches will share more, and if individuals—like you and me—will share more, then we can do it.

The best news is things are already changing. Over the past twenty years the number of children who die before their fifth birthday has been cut in half. Every day nineteen thousand fewer children die of preventable disease. One-third of children who were unable to attend school because of poverty can now be educated. And here is the best part, just thirty years ago, 52 percent of the world's population lived in extreme poverty. Today that number is just 16 percent! "The question is not, 'Can we end poverty?' The question is, 'How can we end poverty?' "[10]

NOT LONG AGO, The Grove had a team of thirty in Malawi. Unexpectedly, after visiting one of the villages that we have a community-to-church relationship with, they felt compelled to dig the village a well for clean water. They had not budgeted for this. The cost to dig the well would be seven thousand dollars. So the team members emailed and Facebooked some friends, and by the next day they had enough money for the project. I shouldn't have been surprised that just thirty Americans had the resources and connections to rally seven thousand dollars in a day.

I started to think, what if every church in America dug just one well a year in Africa? That is more than two hundred thousand wells every year. We would have clean water flowing in every village on the continent in less than a decade.

Together we can end extreme poverty.

We really can.

CHAPTER 10

We Will Stop the Spread of Pandemics

FIRST CONTRACTED MALARIA WHEN I was seven. I cried when I thought I was dying.

Malaria starts with the throbbing headache, the chills, and then the raging fever. It's the fever that will kill you. At first, people from America think it's just the flu. The malaria parasite reproduces rapidly and spreads through your bloodstream. Your body senses the invasion and spikes a fever to kill the intruders. This works momentarily. Your body will kill a large number of the parasites . . . but not all. They take about twelve hours to reproduce millions more. Your fever spikes again, this time higher. Twelve hours later, your temperature will spike even higher. This is when the malaria kills infants and small children. The 106- or 107-degree temperatures are too much. Their vital organs shut down.

The malaria parasite is a relentless demon.

My body ached; my head felt like it was going to bust. I was cold and hot. I was shaking violently with the chill and fever when my mother started me on chloroquine, but I wasn't getting any better. She couldn't hold the fever down. Mom kept wanting me to drink Fanta, but the smell of the Fanta made me want to vomit again.

I couldn't stop shaking. I started to believe I was going to die.

A gathering of tribal pastors crowded around my bed to kneel and pray. This just made me even surer I was going to die in the night and see Jesus. I didn't want to fall asleep, because I knew if I did I would die like our chimpanzee Sadee-Ju, when the army ants ate her while she was sleeping.

I overheard my father talking on his shortwave radio to the bush pilot, asking him how much it would cost to fly me to the capital city of Monrovia where there was a hospital. I'm not sure if it was the money or what, but the plane never came. My mother spent most of that night putting damp washcloths all over my body, trying to calm the raging fever.

Drifting in and out of sleep, I wondered why, if my parents really loved me, they wouldn't send for the bush plane to carry me to the hospital at ELWA in Monrovia. I knew the American doctor there could save me. I knew my body would stop shaking and burning.

They never called for the plane.

I was sick the entire next day. I felt weak. I hadn't eaten in three days. My twin brother, Paul, kept coming in the room and would just stand at the door and look at me. He never said anything; I think he was just checking to make sure I wasn't dead like Sadee-Ju.

Some time, late in the night, the fever broke and I fell asleep.

OVER THE COURSE of my life in Africa I've watched two infectious diseases wreak havoc on the continent: malaria and AIDS. I've watched friends suffer and die. I've performed funerals for the babies whose tiny lives were ended. I've held the orphans of the disease. I've sat with young single mothers whose bodies were ravaged by a sickness they contracted through no fault of their own.

It doesn't have to be this way. We can eradicate malaria; we can stop the pandemic spread of AIDS. But we will have to give our best efforts and pool our resources. With the mass of the tribe, we really can stop them both.

THE FLYING DEMON

AMERICANS ALWAYS ASK the same questions when they hear about children dying of malaria in Africa, "If the Fansidar or chloroquine treatment only costs a dollar, why won't the parents buy the medicine when their children are sick?"

Or, I hear them ask, "The mosquito nets are only five dollars; why won't the parents buy the nets to hang over their children's beds?" What they don't know is that the parents love their children deeply, but sometimes even a dollar is too much money when you have no money at all.

MOSES IS WHY I first asked the tribe at The Grove for a thousand mosquito nets.

I had known Moses for several years in Malawi. He was the mechanic at the college where I taught. I wasn't so surprised when he came into my office to ask for a favor, but I went numb when he told me why he needed my help. He asked if I would buy the coffin for his baby girl.

What made the news really sting was that Moses's six-month-old daughter was a twin, and so was I.

He said it was malaria that stole her life.

My soul ached to the core as I handed Moses enough kwaches for the small coffin.

As he was leaving, I asked, "So how's her twin sister?"

With his head hanging low, his shoulders slumped as he looked up with hollow eyes. "Palmer, she died two weeks ago from the malaria."

I had no idea. I was filled with shame. I saw Moses practically every day, but he never said a word. I still should have known. I wish I had known. If I had known that the girls were sick, I could have bought them Fansidar. I would have bought them nets. But why hadn't I just bought the nets in the first place when the babies were born? I guess I never thought about it. I guess I thought Moses would have bought nets. But I also knew Moses didn't earn very much, and I knew that fathers can't spend money on nets when their families are hungry.

I felt so much shame and anger that day. Shame for not doing more. Shame for not knowing about Moses's twin baby girls dying. Anger that I had done nothing. Anger that malaria is preventable and utterly treatable and completely eradicable.

Every time I return to Malawi we distribute mosquito nets, and I always give Moses a handful—even though I know it's far too late. But I also know that Moses has three more children who need them. What I really wish is that I had the nets to give away when Moses's tiny twin girls needed them most.

HER NAME WAS TROUBLE

SAITOSO MEANS TROUBLE in Chechewa, and that was her name.

I didn't know Saitoso was in trouble when my wife and I first met her. She was working as a waitress at the restaurant in Lilongwe. We liked her perky smile and friendly way. That's why we asked her to babysit our sons.

Shortly after that she complained of bilharzia, so we asked our doctor to treat her. That's when he gave us the news: "You need to tell Saitoso she is HIV positive."

I had never before had to tell someone she was dying. I felt hopeless, useless.

All I can do is tell her she's dying? There has to be more we can do.

WE MUST DO BETTER

ALMOST HALF THE world's population—or 3.3 billion people—is at risk of malaria, and more than 35 million people today live with AIDS.

Malaria and AIDS plague Africa like nowhere else. The conditions are just too perfect for the flying demons that carry malaria. It's an ecological curse. The rain, the humidity, and the high temperatures provide an ideal breeding ground in the swamps and everywhere else during the rainy season. And it's the children and young mothers who are often the innocent victims of AIDS. The silent killer has a death grip on their lives long before they are aware, never having a chance to stop the killer.

But we can.

For centuries malaria has been the leading killer in Africa. It causes poverty. It kills almost a million people every year. Eighty-five percent of those who die from malaria in Africa are children under the age of five. And every year 2.3 million more people contract HIV, a quarter of a million of them also children.

Bed nets and modern medication can go a long way in the battle against malaria and AIDS. With our teams we have delivered thousands of nets to dwellings in Africa, but I have yet to walk into a mud hut that already has even one net.

It's a simple, five-dollar solution.

The frustrating truth is, no one should die of malaria, and no one should go untreated for AIDS! We have the tools and the treatment, and it's unacceptable for so many children and pregnant women to die.

We can do better.

We must do better.

I LOVE THAT everyday, ordinary people like Laurie are taking the initiative.

When Laurie Lathem heard Senegalese rock-star drummer Youssou N'Dour perform, he challenged the audience to do something about the problems of AIDS and malaria in Africa. Laurie says she was compelled to respond. The next day she contacted a nonprofit dedicated to the problem and told them she wanted to hold a drumming-enthusiasts event to raise funds for bed nets in Africa. They loved it. She dubbed the night "Drums to Beat Malaria." Laurie says the night was a hit. A crowd of over two hundred showed up, including film industry professionals, Venice hipsters, lawyers, Rotary Club members, artists, a hedge fund manager, and plenty of Senegalese, who came ready to dance.[1]

THE DEMON IS ON THE ROPES

IT'S TIME FOR the knockout blow.

In general, health experts shy away from the word *eradicate* when it comes to pandemics. It used to be that way when they talked about malaria and AIDS, but not anymore.

The good news is, awareness has increased, and people everywhere are bothered and responding. People like Bill and Melinda Gates are leading the way to stop malaria. I love their optimistic determination: "Eradicating malaria is not a vague, unrealistic aspiration but a tough, ambitious goal that can be reached within the next few decades."[2]

Similarly, change makers like Bono are having an impact on AIDS. Recently Bono's ONE organization launched a revolutionary awareness program they are calling "No Child Born with HIV by 2015." I love the godly audacity of the campaign.

Grammy-winning recording artist Alicia Keys has also joined this battle to rescue infants from the curse of AIDS. She says, "We know how to stop the virus from passing from mother to child. We have the medicine. We have the knowledge. But do we have the will? If we come together, I know that we can do this."[3]

Alicia is spot-on. We have the know-how; we have the money. All we need now is a tribe of people with enough heart to stop the dying.

International funding for the fight against malaria has risen substantially in recent years, reaching about $1.5 billion in 2010, up from $100 million just ten years ago. Over the past decade the number of annual malaria cases globally has fallen by 38 percent, and in forty-three countries the cases have dropped by 50 percent.

Seven countries have recently declared their eradication of malaria. Another ten nations are monitoring transmission and believe that the goal of zero malaria cases is soon within reach.

About ten years ago, the world woke up to the effectiveness of bed nets. Around the globe, countries and organizations rallied to provide more nets. Today, almost four-fifths of sub-Saharan Africa's at-risk population have received bed nets. We're doing better.

The World Health Organization (WHO) has said that nearly a third of the 108 countries affected by malaria are on course to eliminate the disease over the next ten years. WHO's director of malaria programs, Dr. Robert Newman, has said, "The results of the past decade exceed what anyone could have predicted and prove that malaria control is working. Many of these achievements have occurred in the last five years, which tells us that we are becoming increasingly effective in our ability to tackle this disease."[4]

In much the same way, several critical factors have combined to slow the spread of AIDS. First, more readily available and affordable antivirals are keeping young mothers and fathers alive. Second, a host of nonprofits, along with African governments, have led massive campaigns to raise awareness in urban areas. And third, the most surprising factor to many, is that African pastors are talking openly about ways to stop the spread of AIDS. Pastors in places like Lilongwe and Lu-

saka are preaching practical sermons about resisting tempta-
tion, being faithful to your spouse, the issues that result
when spouses withhold sex, the dangers of polygamy, and
the importance of monogamy. Experts acknowledge that
these churches and pastors who talk honestly about the disease are having an impact. Since roughly 90 percent of
sub-Saharan Africans attend church every Sunday, the word
is spreading from village to village and community to com-
munty.[5] Over the past ten years infection rates have declined
by 10 percent.

Researchers and scientists are saying that within five
years, with increased availability of antiretroviral treatments
(ARVs) and universal testing, we can stop the rampant
spread of AIDS. They are saying we can break the back of
the epidemic.

My invitation to the tribe is for all of us to participate in
eradicating these life-threatening diseases. Every effort matters. We need all hoses on the fire.

We need more tribal people like Ben Kingston and Ike
Stranathan, who live in Manhattan Beach. Ike and Ben
started Netting Nations. I love Ben and Ike's story. They say
neither of them had personally suffered from malaria, known
someone with the disease, or even traveled to Africa. "They
were just two guys who saw a huge problem and decided to
do something about it!"[6] They've distributed more than ten
thousand nets in Africa and have begun a "Net Courier" program, sending college students into infected regions to distribute nets and educate the population on what can be
done to curb the spread of malaria.

Two ordinary guys from California see trouble in this world and respond. They've stopped waiting for the UN or Bill and Melinda Gates to put out the fires on their own. They know every hose matters. That's the kind of tribal people this world needs.

People like Perry Jansen. Just out of medical school, Perry and his family moved to Malawi. They were our neighbors and friends, and he was the college's doctor. After just two years of watching AIDS claim one life after another, Perry couldn't take it anymore. Feeling frustrated and helpless, he left the college hospital to found Partners in Hope, a medical work dedicated to giving life to the women, children, and men in Malawi dying of AIDS.

That was ten years ago. Today Perry has 3,500 HIV patients in his care, including 300 children. He has 2,600 Malawians on ARVs. On top of all this, he leads HIV-prevention programs in forty schools.

This is one young, passionate doctor who was not willing to wait for someone else to stop the scourge of AIDS in Africa.

———

PRACTICALLY EVERY FRIDAY Felix made it back to our house from downtown Lilongwe by noon, when my wife, Veronica, cooked homemade hamburgers and french fries for lunch. Felix was a recent graduate of African Bible College in Malawi, where I taught and he worked as the school's purchaser. When we eventually moved our family back to the

United States, I knew it was Felix's friendship I would miss most.

I did. That's why it stung so deep when only two months after we returned my brother called to say Felix was dead. AIDS had robbed Africa of another brilliant young man with a promising future. Paul said he found money under Felix's bed that he was saving up for the plane ticket to attend grad school in America.

I sat in my backyard for much of the afternoon and cried. It really hurt losing a close friend. But I think what hurt most is that I knew he didn't have to die. We have the drugs. We have the answers. We simply are not doing enough.

So many people are already working to stop the spread of these pandemics ravaging an entire continent, but it will take the tribe to finally stamp them out.

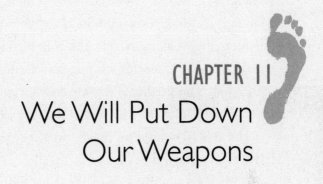

CHAPTER 11
We Will Put Down
Our Weapons

THE AUTOPSY REPORT SAYS THE first-grade girl was shot twenty times by the Bushmaster.

Why are so many people demanding the right to own a Bushmaster automatic rifle? Why all the insisting that people need Bushmasters?

I don't get it.

———

I ESCAPED LIBERIA when the civil war raged and the land filled with guns.

The rebel boy-soldiers loved their guns—and they had plenty of guns. They were led by notorious fighters like General Dragon Master, General Peanut Butter, and General No Mother No Father. The most infamous rebel, however, was General Butt Naked. Reporters dubbed him "the Most Evil Man in the World." General Butt Naked and his ragtag battalion of child-soldiers lived by the gun, looting, raping, and wreaking havoc. Genocide ran rampant. Entire villages were massacred. Some estimate the Most Evil Man in the World killed more than twenty thousand Liberians with his gun.

The rebels' weapon of choice was the American-made M16, even though the AK-47 was cheaper and easier to acquire. They said the Russian-made AK-47 didn't like the rain and swamps and jammed too much. You can't kill so many people when your gun keeps jamming.

Everybody knew the master in the bush was the devil. My Sapo friends would point to the deep bush on the mountain and talk about the devil there. They said that's where the witch doctor and the Grand Devil did their juju in the dark of night. That's where the children were sacrificed to the bush master . . . Satan. General Butt Naked says he was initiated into the "Devil-Bush" (the Liberian term for the Poro secret society) when he was just eleven years old. He says the Grand Devil made him cut the heart from a sacrificed child and eat it. He said he learned to kill when he was small, so when the war started, killing people with the gun was easy.

The boy-soldiers, though, were afraid they would die from the AK-47s and the M16s, so they went to the witch doctor to ask for juju. Sometimes the witch doctor rubbed country medicine on their bodies and told them the devil would make the bullets miss. Some donned wigs and women's nightgowns that flowed when they ran at night to make them look like the spirits in the devil-bush. And the witch doctor told some to fight naked so they would be invisible to the bullet. This was the battalion led by General Butt Naked.

Most people used to describe Liberia as a Christian nation. The nation's founders were Christians. Missionaries flooded the country, and the most remote villages boasted a church. The last president before the bloodshed began, William Tolbert, was even a Baptist minister.

Everything changed when Samuel Doe invaded the executive mansion and murdered President Tolbert with his M16, then named himself *Zoe*—Chief of All Witch Doctors and Grand-Devils.

When Doe—the Zoe—started the killing and the genocide, war spread and the people stopped trusting Jesus and started trusting the master in the bush. The devil.

PRINCE OF PEACE

SHE SAID, "OUR stomachs started to hurt."

That's how the small girl who escaped the massacre at Sandy Hook Elementary School talked about her pain to CNN.

My stomach hurts, too. I'm sickened by the disgusting

killing of children. I'm sick of us not doing a thing to stop all the dying from guns.

So I make an appeal to all: put down your weapons and promote peace.

I know that may sound irrational and fanatical to some, but if you know the Jesus of the Bible then please listen.

When the angels appeared on that first Christmas night they announced, "Peace on earth." Peace is what Jesus came to bring into our world and our personal lives. The ancient prophet Isaiah named him the Prince of Peace. In his first sermon Jesus said, "Blessed are the peacemakers." Then he promised that his peace would remain with us even after he left earth.

When I hear churchgoers say things like, "It's my God-given right to own a gun," or, "If more people had guns these kinds of tragedies would not happen," I wonder when in Jesus' ministry did he ever tell us to take up arms as an answer to the trouble in this world? What does God have to do with your desire to own a gun?

Jesus never said, "Buy more swords at sword shows, because the Romans may attack." He never said, "You need a sawed-off sword or an automatic sword to defend your home." He never said, "Prepare for the end of the world. Buy more swords."

His answer was never weapons.

His answer was always peace.

Jesus' kingdom is a kingdom of peace.

Is the peace of Jesus only something we experience on the inside? Is his peace only for a kingdom after we die?

I say no. The peace of God is for this world—today.

When Jesus was cornered in a dark garden to be crucified and his men drew their swords, he refused to take up weapons.

When Nero began his savage persecution of the early Christians, burning thousands on stakes to light the streets of Rome at night, they refused to take up weapons.

When Martin Luther King Jr.'s youth were attacked by a racist sheriff and his dogs in Montgomery, they refused to take up weapons.

When Nate Saint and four pioneering missioners were attacked and killed by Auca Indians in Ecuador, they refused to take up weapons.

So why do we think followers of Jesus Christ need to take up weapons today?

———

THE FOG OF war still hung heavy in the air when I returned to Liberia after the fighting had stopped.

Peace was precarious.

A cease-fire had been negotiated by a brilliant new president, Ellen Johnson Sirleaf, the first female head of state in Africa. UN checkpoints littered the roads to keep the peace.

But the boys in the bush still had guns.

Lots of guns.

However, the tribal people of Liberia wanted peace. They wanted the killing to stop. They wanted their children to go back to school. They wanted the guns put down.

At the urging of the Liberian government and the United Nations, tribal leaders across the country began asking the boys in the bush to put down their weapons. Their enticement to some was, "Trade your gun for a pair of high-tops."

The guns began to pile up in gritty war-torn towns like Ghanta and Gbanga. Tribal leaders, mothers, and fathers pleaded with their sons, the boy-soldiers, to turn in their weapons—until an entire nation had put down their guns.

Now there is peace.

————

AS I WATCHED the gut-wrenching news of twenty elementary children and six teachers being savagely gunned down in their classrooms, I wondered, *Why do we refuse to put down our guns?*

When two teenagers killed eleven in a Colorado high school in 1999, I thought we would put down our guns.

In 2005, after a sixteen-year-old killed nine people in Minnesota, I hoped we would put down our guns.

Just two years later, after thirty-two were massacred on a university campus in Virginia, I was certain we would put down our guns.

When twelve more were gunned down watching a summer movie in Colorado, I thought there would be a national cry for people to put down their guns.

We the people have been silent.

MY APPEAL IS first to Christ-followers. If you really follow the Jesus of the Bible, then follow his path of peace. Let's put down our weapons and instead become apostles of peace.

Jesus was deeply passionate about peace and ending the violence. His Jewish people wanted him to lead a revolt against the Romans. That's the kind of messiah they wanted. Yet Jesus came as a peace master. That's why he said things like, "I tell you, do not resist an evil person. If someone strikes you on the right cheek, turn to him the other also."[1]

Do you see why I say all this bully talk about home defense and self-protection doesn't come from God?

I hate to say it, but I find the adage "Guns don't kill people; people kill people" intellectually insulting. It makes no sense. It's like saying cigarettes don't cause lung cancer.

I'm not saying don't hunt, if you eat what you kill. But I have to be frank: no one *needs* a semiautomatic weapon, like the ones that have killed so many in movie theaters, shopping malls, and classrooms. If you need a machine gun to kill an unarmed deer, you shouldn't be hunting in the first place. And no one needs the nine-millimeter pistols that kill so many in our inner cities.

The fact is there are simply too many guns lying around our homes and country. Practically once a week I read about children accidentally shooting their mother, their brother, their best friend, or themselves. When will everyone wake up to the madness? Guns are made to kill. The more guns we pack in our closets and cars, the more people will die.

If Jesus was against brutality, violence, and weapons—then so should we.

Our history books are filled with stories of conflict and violence. If there are periods of peace, we don't write much about them. Maybe that's the reason I only recently heard of the WWI Christmas truce.

The British troops said a strange thing happened the night of December 24, 1914. German soldiers began to light candles on their Christmas trees in the trenches! The war was already bloody after just five months of fighting. The trenches were cold, muddy, and smelled of the dead. German families had sent Christmas trees to the front to cheer the soldiers. Bravely, that Christmas night, the young fighters began to light their trees.

Then, from the Christmas tree–lit trenches, the British began hearing the sounds of music. The Germans were singing Christmas hymns! The British applauded and sang their own in return. Then, from across the trenches, they all sang together.

Next, the most stunning thing happened. A few brave Germans crawled out of the filthy trenches and slowly walked toward the Brits, who responded by crawling out of their holes in the mud to meet the enemy. They then exchanged gifts like chocolate and socks, showed each other photographs of their families, and sang Christmas hymns together about peace on earth.

The Christmas truce continued through the next day. The German and British troops organized a soccer match, helped one another bury their dead, and held a Christmas worship service. Some estimate more than a hundred thousand men stopped the fighting to celebrate peace that Christmas day.

But word got back to the generals in Berlin and London that the troops had put down their weapons to have hot cocoa and sing about peace on earth. The generals gave the order to stop the singing and get back to fighting.

We're not so good at peace, at putting down our weapons. We do much better at anger and violence.

I write this at Christmastime, when everyone talks about peace and sings Christmas carols about peace. However, this Christmas, after a mall shooting, a subway shoving, and a massacre in an elementary school, it feels like violence—not peace—fills the earth.

Peace is the great lacking commodity of our culture. I wonder, why is there so much hurting in our world? Why is there so much harming of one another? Why so much abuse? And why so little peace?

I think it's the absence of Jesus—and the abundance of weapons.

When Jesus came he brought a new message, a new way of life, a way of more peace and less violence.

It started when the choir from heaven sang, "Peace on earth."

Sometimes we pursue inner personal peace and become okay with no peace in our world.

My invitation is for you—all of us—to lead the way to peace on earth. It starts with the church, with Christians everywhere. I invite you to pray for peace. Become a promoter of peace. Teach peace. Model peace. Champion peace as a great godly attribute.

My challenge to you is to be an apostle of peace. Spread peace in your workplace and stop the conflicts. Fill your home with words of peace, not shouting and angry words. Bring peace to your friendships, and help end the slander and backbiting.

Jesus' answer to violence was never more violence. Jesus' solution was never retaliation. He said things like, "Love your enemies, do good to those who hate you, bless those who curse you, pray for those who mistreat you."[2] "Put your sword back in its place . . . for all who draw the sword will die by the sword."[3]

What if became famous for peace?

———————

WHEN I CHALLENGE us to be apostles of peace, I think about Sergio Consuegra. Sergio Consuegra is my new hero. Last Sunday Sergio was walking to church in New York City when he witnessed a gang of motorcyclists surround an SUV, smash the windows with their helmets—while cursing and screaming at the couple with their toddler inside—then pull the young father from the car and throw him to the ground. One motorcyclist knifed him while others began punching him and beating his head with their helmets.

In utter disbelief at the scene unfolding in front of his eyes, Sergio rushed in. He said, "I was sure they were killing the man . . . It was like hell, and I had to stop it." He did. He boldly stepped between the bleeding man on the ground and the attackers. With his sermon notebook in hand, he held his arms wide and said, "Stop! Enough!"[4]

Sergio said he felt intense danger, "But I said to myself, I'm not going to move from here . . . even if they hit me."[5] He looked the men square in the eyes and said again, "Enough!"

The violence stopped.

The young father lived.

We need more apostles of peace walking our city streets like Sergio.

THE SOVEREIGNTY OF GOD

I DO NOT make my appeal as any kind of political statement. I'm not asking for any kind of law or vote. This is a moral issue. My position is based on these two simple truths: One, Jesus Christ was morally opposed to violence. Two, I believe in the everlasting sovereignty of God.

The Bible teaches that God is sovereign, meaning he is ultimately in control of all of life. For example, the Psalmist writes, "The Lord will keep you from all harm—he will watch over your life."[6] When the Bible speaks of the sovereignty of God it refers to the fact that God rules and controls everything, that nothing happens outside his direction or plan. Paul the apostle writes, "All things God works for the good of those who love him, who have been called according to his purpose."[7] To say God is sovereign means he holds all the power; nothing happens by mistake. I love the way the psalmist puts it: "Our God is in heaven doing whatever he wants to do."[8]

So if you believe the Bible, then you can have the assurance that your life is in the great hand of God—and not worry about all the self-defense, tough-guy talk.

The prophet Isaiah spoke of the kind of people ruled by God: "They will beat their swords into plowshares and their spears into pruning hooks."[9] What if our churches became the Ghantas and Gbangas of this country and we invited people to lay down their weapons at the foot of the cross as a statement that we want the peace and love of God to rule our lives and families and communities and cities?

What if, instead of exchanging guns for high-tops, we handed out Bibles? Brand-new Bibles for every member of every family who came to put down their weapons. Then we took their weapons to a blacksmith who literally beat them into hoes and shears for the farmers we partner with in places like Haiti, Guatemala, and Liberia.

———————

GENERAL BUTT NAKED no longer goes by his wartime moniker. His name is Joshua Milton Blahyi.[10] Most people just call him Pastor Blahyi. After the war, Joshua the warlord met the Lord. He has spent the last five years asking his enemies to forgive him. He has even offered to go to the Hague to be tried for his war crimes. Now he spends his days running a rehabilitation center for boy-soldiers and pastoring a church that meets in an abandoned military barrack. The license plate on his rusting Mercedes reads Be Holy.

Joshua has put down his weapon and picked up the cross.

If the peace of God can rule the Liberian jungle it can rule anywhere . . . even the cities and suburbs of America.

CHAPTER 12
We Will Promote Sustainability and Care for the Environment

WE STARTED A COMMUNITY GARDEN because ecology matters to this next generation, and ecology matters to God.

God began his work in a garden. When the first two inhabitants walked this planet, he told them to take care of the earth and all he had created. If this was true for Adam and Eve, it holds true for you and me today. One of our great, God-given duties is to care for his world.

Tribal people know that nothing we throw away is ever really gone. They understand that all resources eventually run out, and they want to leave this earth just a little bit better for their children than when they arrived. That's why we planted a community garden at The Grove.

We started a garden because we want to remind people that you can grow. God has put you here to produce something good with your life.

We started a garden so families could cultivate land and turn the soil together to grow produce that would be on their table at night.

We started a garden to share. Every person or family that tends a plot is asked to share a part of their harvest with our Live Love neighborhood, where immigrant families struggle to get their feet on the ground and put food on their table.

We started a garden to remind people that the earth is God's and he wants us to use it wisely to meet our needs and the needs of generations to come.

We started a garden because it creates community and strengthens tribes. In the Sapo tribe, for example, no one hoes alone, plants alone, or harvests alone. Planting and harvesting are always done together. We started a garden, because God wants us to grow.

GREEN IS GOD'S IDEA

I DON'T UNDERSTAND why so many Christians act cavalier toward God's creation, or mock conservation efforts and refuse to take ecology seriously.

This is not just my casual observation; this is what people in and outside the church have seen in the Christian attitude for half a century. In 1967, Lynn White, a professor of history at U.C. Berkeley, wrote an article for *Science* titled, "The Historical Roots of Our Ecological Crisis." White says,

Both our present science and our present technology are so tinctured with orthodox Christian arrogance toward nature that no solution for our ecologic crisis can be expected from them alone. Since the roots of our trouble are so largely religious, the remedy must also be essentially religious, whether we call it or not. We must re-think and re-feel our nature and destiny.[1]

White is right. We must rethink our theological position and end our apathy toward God's creation.

It sometimes seems that we are more concerned with a political stance than with being obedient to God. Ecology is not a political ideal, it's a biblical value.

Why are we leaving issues like ecology to others to be concerned about? Why do we ignore them, acting as though they are not our bother? Why do we breeze by the mountain of scriptures that call us to be people concerned with God's creation?

"Plant and harvest your crops for six years, but let the land be renewed and lie uncultivated during the seventh year." EXODUS 23:10–11

"The land is mine and you are but aliens and my tenants. Throughout the country that you hold as a possession, you must provide for the redemption of the land." LEVITICUS 25:23–24

"They will neither harm nor destroy on all my holy mountain, for the earth will be full of the knowledge of the LORD as the waters cover the sea." ISAIAH 11:9

"Do not pollute the land where you are." NUMBERS 35:33

"Speak to the Israelites and say to them: 'When you enter the land I am going to give you, the land itself must observe a sabbath to the Lord.'" LEVITICUS 25:2

For some reason, few Christians say much about the environment. We act like God doesn't care. I have actually heard people say, "God's going to destroy the planet anyway." This kind of thinking needs to change.

Christians must set the agenda. We are the people who must declare the salvation of God for the cosmos. The church must lead the way for ecological renewal. God has commissioned His people to be the agents through whom He rescues this world from its polluted condition. Let us be faithful.[2]

Christians today must develop a theology of ecology. Some have used the term *eco-theology*.

The goal is to establish and explain the relationship between God, his creation, and his people who live in it.

Eco-theology proposes that a correct view of ecology, as well as a genuine concern for it, is both biblical and important to God. An adequate understanding of God must include an understanding of ecology.[3]

Pollution and the abuse of natural resources destroy the world as God made it. We only have a limited amount of energy, resources, and water on this earth, yet our populations are growing exponentially. Ignoring these limitations is not just ignorant, it's wrong. God's people need to realize that we live in the house of God. We are to care for this house we live in, value it, protect it, and even leave it more beautiful than we found it.

When you stay at a friend's vacation cabin in the mountains, you don't leave dirty dishes in the sink, soiled linens on the bed, muddy boots in the living room, popcorn spilled on the floor. Rather, you try to leave the home better than it was when you arrived. You repair his leaking faucet, shovel the snow, and take your own trash with you.

SUSTAINABILITY

IN RECENT YEARS the term *sustainability* has gained increased recognition and respect.

A widely accepted definition comes from the 1987 UN conference, when it defined sustainable developments as those that "meet present needs without compromising the ability of future generations to meet their needs."[4] It is the balance of reciprocity between a society and its environment so that the population grows without adversely damaging the environment on which it depends.

Sustainability is rooted in the basic principle that everything we need for our living and well-being depends, directly or indirectly, on our environment. It provides a means by which people and the world God created can coexist in a way that is good for both and leave things a bit more beautiful for future generations. Here are a few simple suggestions for you and your tribe:

1. Recycle and reuse.

THIS IS NOT a new idea, but it is one that will not only reduce waste but can also potentially provide additional income. Perhaps start a church-wide recycling program and encourage members to participate as a way, for example, to raise funds to help farmers in Haiti.

2. Turn the thermostat down or up.

TELL YOUR PEOPLE church is going to be just a little less comfortable now. Tell them you're running things just a bit cooler in the winter and warmer in the summer. They'll learn to bring a coat to church in January . . . or wear shorts in June. I realize that for those of you down south, this sounds heretical—the shorts part. Not wearing the khaki trousers and blue blazers for a few months could make things more exciting for everyone.

3. Cycle to work—and church.

WHAT IF WE, Christ-followers everywhere, began to set the conservation standard? What if we helped make our towns and cities famous for their bike trails and bikers . . . even biking to church?

4. Plant a tribal garden.

START A GARDEN in your backyard, or a community garden in your neighborhood or at your church. Or find an abandoned lot in the most blighted part of town and turn a dirty corner into a bit of Eden.

LIVE LIKE FRANCIS

THE TWELFTH-CENTURY MONK Francis of Assisi was one of the first prominent voices for conservation. His message and mantra was that the world was created good and beautiful by God but now needs to be restored and protected because of humanity's sinful practices destroying its natural beauty.

Francis's love for animals is legendary. The Fioretti, a collection of true stories and folklore written about the saint after his death, tells of a day when Francis was traveling with friends. They came upon a place in the road filled with thousands of birds. Francis asked his friends, "Wait for me while I go to preach to my sisters the birds." The birds surrounded him, drawn by the power of his voice. Not one flew away. And Francis preached to them.[5]

Another legend from the Fioretti tells about the city of Gubbio, where Francis lived. There was a terrifying and ferocious wolf roaming the land that attacked people and their farm animals.

> Francis had compassion on the townspeople and went up into the hills with several friends to find the wolf. Soon fear of the wolf caused all his companions to flee, but the saint pressed on alone. When he found the wolf he made the sign of the cross and commanded the wolf to come to him. The wolf closed his jaws and lay down at the feet of St. Francis. Then he scolded him for his behavior, "Brother Wolf, you do much harm in these parts and you have done great evil . . ." said Francis. "All these people accuse you and curse you . . . But, Brother Wolf, I would like to make peace between you and the people."[6]

Francis then led the wolf back to the village, and, surrounded by stunned citizens, he proposed a pact between them and the wolf. The wolf would leave the people and their animals alone, and, in return, the village people would feed the hungry wolf.

We can learn from Saint Francis and realize that God's creation needs our protection and cultivation. We should be bothered when animals go extinct or are killed for sport, not hunger, when whales are needlessly slaughtered, or farm animals abused. A right heart for God will be tender toward God's good and beautiful creation.

TRIBAL GROWING

EVERY SAPO IS an agriculturalist. You really don't have a choice. In the rain forest there is no industry, no retail, no silicon jungle. You better plant, or your family doesn't eat.

The good news is, whatever you plant will grow: cassava, palm nuts, rice, collard greens, yams, mangoes, papaya, bananas. The Sapo people do not go hungry.

In the bush the Sapo literally live off the land. Homes are built with the clay from the swamps. Roofs are thatched with branches from the palms that fill the jungle, and all the food your family needs is grown on your farm.

And the best part is, you never build or plant alone. Tribal farming and growing crops is always a community effort. Only the cockroach lives alone. Liberians have stories that explain why life happens the way it does. One of my favorites is "Why Chicken Eats Cockroach":

Time-O-Time. Time. [That's how you open a story in Liberia, kind of like, "Once upon a time."]

This one time, Cockroach came to Chicken and said, "Let's make our farm together this year. If you help me cut the bush and plant my farm, then I will help you clear, burn, and plant your farm."

Chicken said, "Sure, no problem," because this is the way of the tribe.

For the next three weeks Chicken worked vigorously every day with Cockroach, cutting the bush in the hot sun, hoeing the hard ground, and planting all the rice. Chicken's back was aching, the driver ants were biting, and the saw grass had cut his legs up and down. But finally they were done.

So Chicken said to Cockroach, "Okay, I will meet you in the morning, and now we will start making my farm."

Early in the morning Chicken came to Cockroach's house and started beating on the door, "Bock, bock. Wake up, Cockroach, time to work."

But Cockroach was lazy and wanted to sleep. "I say, Chicken, my head is hurting. Go in the bush and start working, and I will meet you there just now."

Chicken agreed and left. But Cockroach, after he was finished sleeping, went to the village palaver hut and started drinking cane-juice and palm-wine with his friends and playing the drum, singing, "Chicken is a foolish man, oh. He working in the hot sun on my farm and suffering by his one." Then Cockroach would laugh and laugh.

That afternoon when the sun was dimming and the sky was turning dark, Chicken came back to town. He was frustrated that Cockroach never came to work on his farm, but he also understood that maybe he had the malaria that was making his head hurt. But then when he reached the village he heard Cockroach singing and mocking him. He was so vexed he ran straight to the palaver hut and started chasing Cockroach. "You are a lazy man! When I catch you I will stab you with my beak!"

That's why, today, whenever a chicken sees a cockroach, it will always chase the cockroach, trying to end its dirty life.

The Sapo tribe takes community gardening seriously.

AND SO DOES this next tribe of Christ-followers.

Target Earth International is an organization dedicated to helping Christians understand and promote care for the earth. They are teaching people how to actively engage in protecting endangered species, reforesting, helping the poor grow more food—and sharing the love of Christ.

They lead college students across the country and around the world to help heal what people have destroyed. Brenna Moore served with Target Earth International while she was a college student. Brenna says as she gave her summer to re-planting trees she realized many Christian college students were "either really into environmental issues or way into the Christian faith, but they're not really making connection be-tween personal faith and social issues."[7] Despite this dispar-ity, though, more and more people are starting to realize the deep-rooted connection between faith and ecology.

Christian leaders and educators are also realizing that the church can no longer ignore environmental issues. Jona-than Merritt, author of *Green Like God*, writes, "If we are concerned about the gospel, we should be concerned about the environment. While the two issues might not immediately strike one as connected, I have come to believe they are inextricably so."[8]

The bottom line is this: the tribe will not embrace a Christianity that is environmentally abusive, or even environmentally ambivalent. And the truth is, the concern is biblical. The church of tomorrow will flourish only when we begin to take matters of ecology seriously.

God spoke:
"Let us make human beings in our image,
make them reflecting our nature
So they can be responsible for the fish in the sea,
the birds in the air, the cattle,
And, yes, Earth itself."[9]

CHAPTER 13
We Will Live Simply

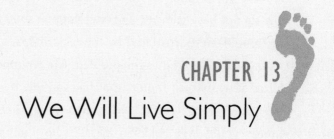

THE PEOPLE OF THE SAPO tribe have never heard of a storage unit. In fact, I've yet to walk into a hut that even has a closet. And, of course, no one needs a garage either.

Most of my neighbors here in the American burbs can't park their cars in their three-car garages. They have too much stuff.

STORAGE WARS

MY FRIEND BRET knows a man named Mr. Knuppe. In the 1960s Mr. Knuppe was building apartments in the Bay Area around San Francisco. Apartments are cramped and usually do not have garages, and Mr. Knuppe soon noticed that his renters were frustrated by the lack of space for all their stuff. As he looked into the problem Mr. Knuppe says he realized it wasn't just renters that had too much stuff; in fact, most Americans were acquiring more possessions than their homes could ever hold. So in 1970 he purchased a small piece of land in Alameda and built California's first self-storage. People in California told Mr. Knuppe he was nuts. They said, who will ever pay money just to use a ten-by-ten shed to store stuff? Nobody has that much stuff, they said.

In just a few weeks he rented out all the units he owned, so he opened another in Berkeley, then San Pablo, Vallejo, San Leandro, Foster City, Colma, and Hayward. Soon Mr. Knuppe owned thousands of storage units up and down the California coast. He made millions simply giving people a place to store their stuff.[1]

We like our stuff.

Recently, a new commercial building went up across the street. The sign said Watermark. The architecture was modern and progressive. I pictured the space filling with French restaurants and day spas. When it opened, the entire thing was a storage unit. They say it's air-conditioned.

For our stuff?

I've always wondered what fills the forty-six thousand

storage facilities in America (worldwide there are only another twelve thousand), but now there's *Storage Wars,* so now I know. It's junk. A lot of dusty LPs, treadmills, and cheap laminate furniture. Once in a while on the TV show the buyers find something valuable. People say the producers salt the lockers with expensive items. I believe it. Because really, who would ever leave an Andy Warhol original in a dirty storage unit in San Bernardino?

The king of wisdom, Solomon, was honest enough to say, "I hated all the things I had toiled for under the sun, because I must leave them to the one who comes after me."[2]

Jesus used to talk about how ludicrous it was to store stuff on earth: "Don't store up treasures here on earth, where moths eat them and rust destroys them, and where thieves break in and steal. Store your treasures in heaven, where moths and rust cannot destroy, and thieves do not break in and steal. Wherever your treasure is, there the desires of your heart will also be."[3]

He is right. Our hearts follow our stuff.

Like Jesus says, storing up on earth is useless. We should have learned from the pharaohs. They built the largest storage units the world has known, but they still couldn't take their stuff with them. Worse, it all wound up being looted by tomb raiders.

It's the same for us. We can keep storing up stuff. We can keep the best for ourselves. We can buy the baddest car and the biggest house and the coolest clothes, but it all stays on this side of heaven. Instead, we should live simply and live generously. Because if you don't, the Saturday morning after you die everything's going up for sale on your front lawn. Everything. Your Tommy Bahama shirts, your Express outfit, your socket set and rusty hubcaps, your iPhone and iPad, your Sub-Zero fridge, your Ugg boots and Croc shoes, your True Religion jeans, and your sixty-five-inch 3-D plasma TV. And whatever doesn't sell on Saturday, your brother-in-law from Des Moines is putting on eBay on Sunday.

SIMPLE THINGS

VALUE AUSTERITY

In our down economy, austerity has become the new buzzword. Companies, governments, and even families are ready to live with less. That's how this tribe wants it. They buy organic foods, wear vintage clothing, recycle, bike to work, and shop less. I like the plaque hanging in our friend Amy's home that reads Live Simply.

Increasingly, this next generation of Christ-followers are intentionally making simplicity a way of life. Mike Foster leads just such a tribe. He calls it the Junky Car Club. Mike says he was living the So Cal dream—driving a slick sports car with a fat payment—when it hit him. "This is stupid. I'm wasting so much money."[4] So he traded in the money guzzler for a 1993 Toyota Camry with 150,000 miles, a cracked windshield, and a broken AC. Mike then started giving away the money he saved every month to organizations such as Compassion that help heal broken people and places.

Now Mike invites others to join this tribe that takes pride in driving junky cars (he calls it Junk Pride) so they can give more to others. Our culture says, "You are what you drive." Mike says he likes that, because when you drive an affordable car you can live more generously.

———

I THINK THE problem is we try to hold on to too much. We are like the vervet monkeys of the Kalahari. When the bushmen want to catch a vervet, they carve a small hole in a gourd, drop a rock in it, then tie the gourd to a tree. From above, the curious monkeys have watched the whole thing. As soon as the bushman walks away, the monkey scampers down the tree, crams his fist through the hole, and grabs on to the rock—but now that he has made a fist he can't pull his hand out. As the bushman comes back to capture his prey, the monkey will scream and dance wildly, trying to break free from the gourd, but he won't let go of the treasure in his fist—a worthless rock.

We are like that, aren't we?

We hold on too tightly.

Back when I was a college pastor, a couple in my ministry asked me to fly to Colorado to perform their wedding. No problem. Until, right after the ceremony, I realized I still needed a ride to the airport, about an hour away—at 5:00 a.m. the next morning.

I started with the father of the bride. He said he had plans. Next, I asked the father of the groom. He was flying out that night. Then I went through everyone I had met over the course of the weekend: uncles, brothers, cousins— all no's.

At midnight, I finally went back to the home where I was staying with several of the groomsmen. They all had reasonable—if somewhat lame—excuses. Five in the morning is stinkin' early for college guys. I knew one last guy was still out, so I put a short note on his door explaining that I was trying to make it back to L.A. to lead my college ministry the next morning, then went to bed.

At 2:30 a.m. he knocked on my door and said with a smile, "I'll be glad to take you."

"You will? Dude, we have to leave in, like, two hours. Are you sure?"

"Bro, I have to take you," he said matter-of-factly.

"Why do you say you have to?"

"Palmer, it's not my car; it's God's car. The first thing I did when I bought my truck last year was pull over on the side of the road to tell God this was his truck. If he ever needed his truck for any reason, it was his. So, when you, a pastor, a man of the cloth, asks me to take you to the airport—I must take you."

That is such a biblical view of stuff. The psalmist writes, "The earth is the Lord's, and everything in it."[5] So, ultimately, stuff is not mine or yours.

Hold on loosely.

SHARE EVERYTHING

THE AVERAGE AMERICAN owns nineteen pairs of shoes, three TVs, two cars, and ten credit cards. The storage unit business is a $22-billion-a-year industry, with more than seven hundred new facilities opening annually; that outpaces McDonald's. I guess we like our junk even more than our junk food.

I invite you to pause here and consider something a little fanatical: *forty days of simplicity.* Over the next forty days would you be willing to buy less and give more? A Lent of sorts. My challenge to you for this period is to stop buying more clothes, more electronics, more home decor, more golf clubs . . . more of anything that you and your family do not need to survive. And each day over the same forty days find something to give away. Because the truth is we all live with excess. Our closets, garages, and storage units have an excess of T-shirts, appliances, computers, sports equipment, tools, furniture, and shoes.

I say all of this with the hope that we will realize we don't need so much stuff and that these forty days will turn into an entirely new lifestyle.

Declutter your life.

Live with less.

Share more.

When I hear Christians say things like, "I can't help (in places like Haiti); I'm broke," I wish their eyes would open to how much they really do have to give. The truth is, we have a hundred times as much as most others in the developing world. We are a blessed people.

We can't share much, though, if we are keeping so much for ourselves. That's why Jesus kept saying to live simply. "You cannot become my disciple without giving up everything you own."[6]

In Robert Fulghum's *All I Really Need to Know I Learned in Kindergarten,* he puts at the top of his list: share everything. That's the best kind of life. Jesus said, "Give away your life; you'll find life given back, but not merely given back—given back with bonus and blessing. Giving, not getting, is the way."[7] When you share, when you give, you become the fortunate one.

The question is, will you turn your blessing into a blessing for others?

WITH HAIR CROPPED high and tight, and visibly fit, it is easy to tell Rod's a former U.S. Army Ranger. Walking out of church a few Sundays ago, Rod stopped me to tell me about his wife's experience in Malawi. She had just returned with our team giving medical care to sick mothers and children in remote villages, giving hope to desperate communities, giving five thousand plus pairs of shoes to barefoot farmers and schoolkids, and giving away the love of Jesus.

"Palmer, you need to know how much this experience has meant to my wife and our family," Rod began. "She's not the same person anymore . . ." His voice trailed. He couldn't say another word. I could tell he had much more to say, but his eyes were welling with tears and his throat tightened. Rod the Army Ranger just walked away.

Two Sundays later I saw Rod in the courtyard. He rushed over with a great big smile. "Sorry about that the other day, Palmer. What I wanted you to know is that my wife is not the same person anymore—" Then he stopped. He couldn't speak. Rod the Ranger walked away again.

I know now what Rod was trying to tell me. His wife, Rebecca, says that before leaving for Africa their family had been through four years of hell dealing with an emotionally abusive situation for their daughter at school. Rebecca was exhausted and in much need of a break. As she contemplated whether or not this was a good time to serve in a faraway place, Rod said to her, "You are not meant to walk in the pain of the past anymore; you are meant to walk in Malawi."

So she did. It took all kinds of sacrifice—financial, work, family—for Rebecca to travel to Africa to bless others, but now she says she's the blessed one. She talks about how while giving healing to broken people in Malawi, her own brokenness was healed.

I think many of us forget that the best life is the generous life. The most fortunate life is the life lived for the good of others. When you give your stuff—and your life—away *you* become the blessed one.

Jesus was right when he said, "It is more blessed to give than to receive."[8]

THE BEST PLACE to store your stuff is heaven.

That's what Mr. Knuppe has started to do. He's now in his seventies and has begun to give away more than he keeps. My friend Bret is a church planter in Las Vegas. His new church needed to move out of a strip mall and into a church home. Bret knew Mr. Knuppe well enough to ask if he would lend the start-up money they needed to build— eleven million dollars!

Mr. Knuppe gave them the loan.

When they started building, I asked Bret, "That's a pretty big loan. How much interest are you paying?"

"I don't know," Bret answered. "Mr. Knuppe never said much about interest."

"Well, what are the terms then? When do you have to pay him back?"

"I don't know," Bret said again. "He never mentioned that either."

I've often wondered why Mr. Knuppe isn't so interested in interest or when he will get his money back. I think it's because he's more interested in treasure in heaven than treasure in storage units.

CHAPTER 14
We Will Create More Art and Make the World Beautiful

THE MODERN CHURCH HAS LONG had a strained relationship with the artist. Like the Taliban that destroyed the art in the Bamiyam Valley, our clergy of the twentieth century smashed the stained-glass windows of our churches and put the artwork and crosses in the Dumpster, while theologians used twisted proof texting to push artists to the fringes of modern Christianity.

But that was yesterday. In the tribal church of tomorrow, artists lead the way—the creatives, the innovators, and the beat poets speak the theology of this generation. We can try to ignore them or dismiss their presence as a trend, but we will lose—lose the ability to reach this culture in this moment. Lose the opportunity to reclaim the biblical values of wonder and awe.

We can keep preaching poorly interpreted theology from Leviticus that tattoos are an abomination and that art becomes an idol. However, this generation has left behind those tired and false propositions. The God-passioned artists of today have turned their canvases into the Wittenberg cathedral door of 1517. With each stroke of their brushes, they write a new ninety-five-point thesis.

They use color and melodies and prose to protest the dispassion of the church. They say their art is a voice for all who have been silenced.

Here is what we have missed. The artist brings a quality of wonder and awe for God that is not found in our systematic theology texts. They reawaken us to the invisible qualities, mystery, and paradox of God. In the modern era, the church reduced worship to stale music droned from the pages of molding books—the dirge of instruments long forgotten by society—as if their sheer ancientness somehow made them divine. This next generation of Christians refuses to play along with the charade.

The tribe beats a new drum.

CULTURAL ARTISTS

THERE ARE CERTAIN kinds of people who believe they can make the world better and more beautiful. When they look at the trouble all around they don't see hopeless impossibility, they see a canvas waiting to be painted. They picture the way things ought to be, then start to paint the world anew.

Isn't that the test of the true artist? The gifted artist does not simply paint what she sees. The challenge of art is to imagine what is not visible, to picture in the mind something more beautiful—the way it ought to be.

In a way it's the difference between the amateur photographer, who can only take pictures of the way things are, and Van Gogh, who, with a paintbrush, could transform a banal starry night over a sleepy village into a vibrant landscape of raging color and compelling imagery.

LIFE IS BEAUTIFUL

GOD WANTS TO do more than simply fix what is broken in our lives. He wants to make it beautiful.

I have heard it said that during the Renaissance the church saved the arts. For many years, through the Dark Ages, art was banned from sacred places. Art was viewed as secular, or worse, from the devil. But during the Renaissance the church gave new birth to art. Artists were invited into places of worship to transform gray cathedrals into places of beauty.

This period of new birth left us stunning frescos by Michelangelo and the stirring works of Rembrandt, who later became known as the painter of the soul. Countless pieces were painted into the plaster of cathedral walls and carved into the facades of churches. What the Renaissance did best was remind us that life with God is beautiful.

But that was more than half a millennium ago. A strange thing happened in the modern church—art was stripped away. Stained glass was replaced with Plexiglas. Paintings were pulled off the walls in the belief that people would be tempted to pray to the images on canvas. Sheetrock and stucco walls were painted beige. Crosses were stored in closets or tossed into Dumpsters. And most churches in the seventies were built without windows. I have no idea why—perhaps to get better resolution from the overhead projector. What went wrong?

Recently I was in a small Presbyterian church in Aliceville, Alabama, for my brother's ordination service. During practically the entire service I found myself staring at the magnificent stained-glass windows. They were absolutely stunning. Tear them down because someone may pray to them?

When The Grove was in its infancy as a start-up church (hauling chairs, staging, and a sound system in and out of a junior high gym every Sunday), someone donated two pieces of art. They were tapestries with images of Jesus. In one, he holds a child. In the other he holds a sheep. They were by no means fine art—purchased at a local Christian bookstore, I think. However, that was all we had, so we hung them up front each Sunday.

After a few weeks of the "art" (using the term quite freely here) hanging up front, a man approached me to say he was unhappy with it. "You need to take the tapestries down, Palmer."

"Why?" I asked, a little amused.

"Because the Bible says we shouldn't hang art," he stammered.

"No, it doesn't," I countered. Now I was slightly perturbed. "You're making that up."

"Right here in Exodus," he said as he opened his Bible to a page he had already marked. "'You shall not make for yourself an image in the form of anything in heaven above or on the earth beneath or in the waters below. You shall not bow down to them or worship them.'"

"Hold on," I countered. "It says not to bow down and worship. Nobody is worshipping our tapestries."

"Yeah, but they might be tempted to worship them," he argued back.

"That's absurd. No one is going to worship our pictures of Jesus from the Christian bookstore!"

"Well, if you don't take them down, I'm leaving the church," he threatened.

The tapestries stayed.

The Exodus man left.

Today, art hangs on practically every wall at The Grove. Our hallways have become galleries of art. A tribe of artisans has formed. We even have a stained-glass artist who is making The Grove more beautiful.

THIS EMERGING GENERATION has a fundamental appreciation for the arts. Churches that realize this and incorporate art, value art, and promote art are discovering a new connection with the next generation.

The cultural prophet Leonard Sweet writes: "The post-modern renaissance will be led by artists who love God. Is your church celebrating the artisans in its midst? Have you turned your corridors and classrooms into art galleries where your artisanship can be displayed?"[1]

And please don't say, "Only hang art in your church and home if it's *Christian* art." I don't believe any such dichotomy exists. I don't see a distinction between Christian art and secular art. If anything is beautiful, it is beautiful because God made it that way. Are there Christian petunias and secular petunias? Religious peacocks and nonreligious peacocks? Of course not. In the same way, when a piece of art, music, or poetry is beautiful, it's because God made it that way.

Art is important to Christianity, because it so poignantly reminds us of the beauty of the kingdom. God takes dark canvases and colors them. Last Easter I invited Clifton, an artist at The Grove, to paint the Christ during our Easter morning services. He started with a dark canvas—the appropriate background for a lifeless messiah—and a dank gray cave. But by the close of the service his canvas had transformed to a garden scene full of life and light and color, and the risen Christ.

Do you see how art tells the story of the human soul?

PAINT DROPS ON DARK CANVAS

GOD DOES HIS best work on dark canvas.

One of my favorite pieces of art that hangs in our home is Vincent van Gogh's *Starry Night*. Understand, it is not an original. Not long ago, Veronica and I were in New York when we walked by the front doors of MoMA (Museum of Modern Art). She insisted we go in. But I hesitated, because it was thirty-five bucks a pop.

"Palmer, they have *Starry Night*. Don't you want to see *Starry Night*?" she urged. I did, but not for seventy dollars. Instead, I talked her into the nine-dollar poster a guy was selling on the street.

Van Gogh was in his midthirties when he lived the Bohemian life of an artist in Paris and started going mad. Some believe his habit of sipping turpentine and sucking on the ends of his brushes covered in lead-based paint was poisoning him and causing dementia.

A series of events seemed to confirm Van Gogh was not well. First, he attacked his roommate, fellow artist Paul Gauguin. Later, he cut off his own ear, then walked to the bar down the street where he tried to present it as a gift to a young woman named Rachel. He calmly said to her, "Keep this object carefully."

You can understand why, in 1889, Van Gogh's brother had him admitted to the Saint-Paul-de-Mausole asylum in Saint-Rémy.

In spite of being confined to an insane asylum, Van Gogh continued to paint. In the evenings he sat in the garden overlooking the village and painted furiously. His most stunning work from Saint-Rémy is *Starry Night*.

The religious establishment had rejected Van Gogh's art. It was too unique, too nontraditional. He was excommunicated. He was wounded and scarred. In many ways *Starry Night* mirrors his mind and emotions at the time. Colors swirl and seem to jump off the canvas. Everything in the work reflects a tortured and abandoned soul.

Van Gogh painted everything of God disproportionately large—the enormous evergreen, the massive moon, the oversized stars. Everything created by people, on the other hand, he painted small and dark. Hurt by the religious institution, he painted the windows of the village church black like the hole in his soul.

Van Gogh's painful rejection by the religious establishment is not an isolated incident from centuries past. Unfortunately, this kind of judging and rejection still happens today. If the future church is going to thrive, though, we must embrace the creatives, the nonconformists, the misfits—and the artists.

Like Van Gogh, the ancients knew that separation from God was hell. That's why we recite lines from the Apostle's Creed like, "[He] was crucified, died, and was buried. He descended into hell . . ." They chose the most godforsaken place to describe Jesus' time in the cave away from God. But here's what happened while Jesus laid in blackness. God covered the world with grace and forgiveness and hope and new life. In the darkest of all moments, God painted the world with beauty. That's when he does his best work.

Like paint drops splattered on a dark canvas, God wants you to paint this world like heaven.

Empower more artisans

I LOVE HOW Melody and Dave Murray have done just that, connecting art with sustainability and social entrepreneurship. They are transforming lives and communities in Nepal for Jesus Christ through textiles and guitars.

When Mel and Dave moved to Rajpur just a few years ago, Mel launched a fashion company called Joyn. She began bringing in women off the streets to carve wooden blocks for printing on fabric, to make art on textiles. Her products are beautiful and fashionable. My friend Esther says she's like a modern-day Mother Teresa.

Dave's passion, on the other hand, is music and guitar making, so he launched Dehradun Guitar Company to craft guitars. Dave recruits and teaches Tibetan artisans how to make some of the finest guitars in India.

Mel and Dave say their goal is to help the poor sustain their families, the impoverished become artisans, the trapped become tradesmen, and the marginalized find dignity.

Dave says his young artisans sing as they build musical instruments.

Something very transformational really is happening.

Compose more poetry

LIFE IN SYNC with God is like poetry. It is like words on a page that roll effortlessly together to rhyme and sing.

Don Miller describes theologian John Sailhamer's knowledge of the Old Testament as "ferocious." I love it. I hope one day someone will so much as say, "Palmer's knowledge of Philemon is ferocious." Sailhamer explains that the Bible is filled with poetry. And often, when the authors of the Bible, like Moses, ran out of words to describe their feelings for God they would break into music and poetry.[2] Language was too limiting, so the writer would tap into the language of the heart. Moses does this. David, of course, does this in the Psalms. So do Joel, Isaiah, Solomon—and the list goes on.

In our analytical, linear-minded Western orientation, we believe we can convince people of truth with well-structured reason and logical conclusions. But truth is often pointless if you haven't captured the heart. Poetry is the language of the soul. Some things in life are simply too complicated, mysterious, and deep for words . . . like eternity, beauty, or love.

Maybe Solomon did it the best. His poetic lines would buckle the knee and melt the heart of any woman.

How beautiful you are, my darling!
With one glance of your eyes you have stolen my heart.
How much more pleasing is your love than wine
And the fragrance of your perfume than any spice!
Your lips drop sweetness as the honeycomb.[3]

In some distant metaphysical way, I think poetry is a picture of how the kingdom-life is meant to be. When you live in harmony with God, life is sweeter. Life works better. Living out the kingdom is not simply a nice idea; it changes the texture of your world. When God is in the prose of your daily rhythm, wives show more affection to their husbands, fathers are more patient with their sons, friends forgive more quickly, restaurant patrons show more grace to their servers.

Life may not be perfect, but it can be poetic.

Live more musically

LIVE MORE MUSICALLY. That's Starbucks's line. The cultural icon realized early on that "when the music stops, life stops." They say you may go for the coffee, but you'll stay for the experience. Because they value music, Starbucks has become a music media giant, selling millions of CDs a year.

Music is a powerful reminder of how beautiful life is with God. At The Grove, we are inviting our people to create more music—compose, play, record, produce. We believe that if God has given a person the beautiful gift of music, they should express and share it with others.

Not everyone agrees with this.

When I taught at a Christian college in Africa a few years ago, a guest pastor from the Deep South was invited to speak for a week in the chapel services. After our worship team and band led a time of singing, I invited him up to speak.

But something was wrong. The man from Mississippi was visibly agitated. His face was as red as his hair.

After traveling nine thousand miles from Mississippi to Malawi, the first words he chose to speak were, "Your happy clappy music does not please God." I was shocked. I couldn't believe he was actually criticizing the worship music we had just finished singing. He continued, "This music you have been singing does not glorify God. If you want to sing correctly you need to sing from this book." He held up a hymnal as red as his face and waved it like a flag, saying, "Your singing is an insult to God. All of this clapping and dancing needs to stop."

My heart broke. Serving as the college's chaplain for the previous two years, I had encouraged the worship team to include more Chichewa music. Whenever their music went from a Western hymn or chorus to a Chichewa song, the contrast was stunning. The decibel level went through the roof, people clapped to the drumbeat, and everyone danced.

For too many decades Malawian Christians were told not to compose. The dominant denomination forbade churches from singing songs that were not in the hymnal. The problem, however, was that all the songs in the hymn book were imported from the West. And if Christianity was going to be authentic to the Malawian, it would need to touch the rhythm of their souls.

This hotheaded pastor's message was a curse and a lie. The Bible repeatedly invites God's people to sing a new song. David the musician king writes, "I will sing a new song to you, my God."[4] Music is the language of the heart, not something to be imported from one particular culture.

I find it insulting to the *imago Dei* when some churches will only sing choruses that are contemporary rearrangements of old hymns—as though hymns are some kind of sacred icon. Don't miss what I am saying; I love hymns. But God did not stop giving beautiful music to his people a hundred years ago. It is sheer ignorance to act as if ancient hymns bear more spiritual weight than a song composed by Josh Havens, or JJ Heller, or Matt Hammitt, or Gil Sandoval . . . or any person anywhere who loves God.

So write more lyrics.

Compose more melodies.

God is not done making music.

———

THE SOURCE OF human creativity is God himself. By his very nature God is creative. Everything God touches reflects his creativity: the universe, the beauty of this world, the complexity of life. And you are his masterpiece in it all, Paul writes. So live out the creative that resides in every person. God wants to use your creativity and art to tell his story—and your story. Art moves people—and moves people to action.

You have a certain set of skills that are unique to you. When you create you bring glory to God. Your creativity makes him known.

I invite you to give God your best: your best *ideas*, your

best *ability,* your best *thinking,* your best *talent,* your best *effort,* and your best *days.*

Live more creatively.

The world is your canvas.

Color it for him.

CHAPTER 15
We Will Love
Like Christ—Always

THEY WERE PASSING AROUND A book of letters when I was hired. It was a large church, a respected church, even named by *Christianity Today* as the "Church of the Year." But now someone had compiled enough letters of complaints about the pastor to literally bind into a book. And the book of hate was being smuggled to adult Sunday-school classes between worship services, like a Pamela Anderson poster in a junior high boys' bathroom.

In another church an obscenely wealthy man pounded our lunch table. He threated to leave, with his money, if he wasn't made an elder.

In yet another church, elders accused the pastor of being like Hitler, so they fired him. Then they made the decision to not replace him, because they didn't want another Hitler. They quickly cut the church's attendance in half, and they think it's working.

Why so much anger and hate in the church? Why so much infighting and backbiting? Why all the gossip and slander that destroys reputations and careers and breaks the spirits of good people? Why have we become okay with this kind of sin?

The Old Testament writers continually wrestled with the question of what kind of spirituality pleases God. Isaiah writes, "You do as you please and exploit all your workers. Your fasting ends in quarreling and strife, and in striking each other with wicked fists. You cannot fast as you do today and expect your voice to be heard on high."[1]

All the dissension and division is killing our worship; it's killing the church. Isaiah is saying, you've got it wrong.

It has to change.

SO THIS PASTOR in the Northwest is getting a lot of press for telling people, "God hates you."

He's wrong.

But, for some reason, he has a large following. I didn't get it until my friend Zach Lind explained that this angry pastor is like the big brother a junior-higher takes to school to stick up for him. He represents a brand of theology that is hostile and divisive. His deductive reasoning and use of scripture may be pathetic, but people are rallying around him, Zach says, because he's their school-yard bully. Blowing hard. Puffing his chest and stomping around onstage instead of on a playground. That's why he has such a following.

Zach's right.

Of all the things Christians are known for—buildings, being right, doctrine, voting along party lines—what Christians must *become* known for most is our love.

Recently I was told someone had complained about our church and said they were leaving. This was the stone they chose to throw on their way out: "He preached too much about love."

I relished the criticism.

Of all the things we are about, of all the things we do, we must be known for love. That's how Jesus said it: "Love God and love others."[2] That's how Paul said it: "The greatest of these is love."[3]

THE TRUTH ABOUT GOD'S LOVE

GUESS HOW MUCH I love you? That's the question Sam McBratney asks in his tender book for kids.[4] Little Nut-Brown Hare keeps asking Big Nut-Brown Hare to guess how much he loves him. He stretches his arms wide to exclaim, "I love you this much!" But no matter how much Little Nut-Brown Hare loves Big Nut-Brown Hare, Big Nut-Brown Hare always loves him more.

I read the words often to each of my sons as they grew bigger. But now they're very big, fifteen and older, so they won't sit still long enough for me to read stories. Now I just tell them how much I love them. Veronica buys the book for practically every friend who has a new baby. They are words we all need to hear.

That's how your father in heaven loves you.

THE CROSS IS the ultimate gesture of love; it's where failure and forgiveness meet. It is where mistakes and grace come together. That is what Jesus wanted Peter to understand as they sat by the charcoal fire.

Of all the things God wants of you, I think it's your heart he desires most. Educators talk about this as the affective component of our faith. The Hebrew people use the heart to describe the seat of our souls' connection to God.

John writes about this moment on the beach by the fire when Jesus sat down with Peter. The last time Jesus had seen Peter was at a distance, across a courtyard where he was still within earshot to hear Peter adamantly deny knowing him. His words hurt the heart of the Christ.

My guess is Peter's heart was messed up. I'm sure it was his idea to go fishing, to get his mind off his failure. John writes that Jesus finds him still in a boat.

"Did you catch anything, children?" I think he was good-naturedly taunting the disciples, something like, "Hey, rookies."

"Try again," he shouts. This is a "try again" story, isn't it? They do, and they catch piles of fish. Suddenly it dawns on Peter that the messiah is back. He jumps out of the boat.

That's when John writes about the charcoal fire. You have to wonder if John mentions it on purpose, because it was by a charcoal fire in Pilate's courtyard where things began to spiral for Peter. I think the charcoal fire is for everyone whose heart is messed up.

Then Jesus asks the question that will cut Peter to the core. It's the question of a lifetime. It's the question of *life*.

But before I mention the question Jesus asked, let's first think about the questions he did not ask:

Why'd you do it?

WE ALL ASK this question when the people we care about do the really wrong things—when they mess up life.

I write this just after watching Dustin Johnson be eliminated from the U.S. Open for absentmindedly letting his club touch the sand in a bunker on the eighteenth hole. I wanted to scream right through the TV, "Why in the world did you ground your club in the bunker? Why'd you do it, Dustin?"

Sin is like blunders in golf; it makes no sense. He knew better!

But this is the absurdity of sin. That's why Alvin Plantinga says, "Sin is foolish."

I think Jesus knows how dumb sin makes us, so he doesn't even ask.

What's wrong with you?

AT TIMES I'VE blurted this out at my sons in frustration.

Veronica inevitably interrupts me and says, "Palmer, there's nothing wrong with him . . . it was a mistake."

A few weeks ago I interrupted my high-schooler's nap on the couch to tell him it was his turn to mow the lawn. Under great duress he finally went out to cut the grass. After he was done I picked up the hose to wash my car, only to notice that my hose was cut in half, actually shredded in half. I looked at it for the longest time trying to figure out what in the world had happened to it. Then it hit me: my son had run over my hose with the mower!

I was steamed when I walked back into the house. "You cut my hose in half!"

"Yeah, I know," he responded rather casually.

"Didn't you see it?!"

"Yeah, I saw it . . . but I thought the mower would clear it."

Now do you see why I've sometimes asked the "What's wrong with you?" question?

But Jesus never asks this question. Because in this world, in this body, there's something desperately wrong with all of us. Jesus knew this. He already knew what was wrong with Peter . . . He needed a savior.

Veronica says I can't ask the "What's wrong with you?" question anymore. She says I hurt my sons' hearts.

She's right. I've stopped asking it.

Do you promise to never do it again?

JESUS WAS SMARTER than most parents. We often insist our kids make promises they can't keep.

"You left your bike in the driveway. Promise me you'll never do it again!" Of course they'll tell you what you want to hear; you look really mad. But they know darn well it's probably going to happen again.

Jesus never asked Peter to make a promise he couldn't keep.

It's not our promises God wants most.

The one question Jesus does ask is:

Do you love me?

I THINK HE asks this because that's what God really wants: your heart, your love. He's not asking for cheap promises. He's not looking for a greater effort. He doesn't even wait for your apology.

Now know this: "Do you love me?" is a very risky question. When you ask this question you open your heart. It's like asking a girl out to a very nice restaurant. You finally work up enough courage to lean across the table, look deep into her eyes, and mumble, "I love you."

It's a risk, a great risk.

Because what if it's just crickets? Or what if she just looks back at her menu and blurts, "I'll have the steak béarnaise; I like cheese."

When you ask the "Do you love me?" question, you leave your heart wide-open.[5]

But with that risk comes the possibility of great reward. Because if they love you back, everything changes.

Have you ever wondered why Jesus kept asking Peter the same question? Some try to say it's because Peter denied him three times. Some say it was because he had been dead for three days. Others say he changed the phrasing in Aramaic and there's some underlying meaning. Maybe.

I think Jesus kept asking the same question because Peter's words were so good to hear. "You know that I love you."

I think we forget that our God is a very relational God. And, like you and me, he longs to hear the words *I love you*!

He's asking you and me the same question. He wonders where our hearts really are:

- Do you really love me? Because you seem to care more about entertainment and pleasure than me.

- Do you really love me? Because it seems like your heart's not in it.

- Do you really love me? Because you keep doing the things that really hurt me.

So do you really love God? Honestly? Has he really stolen your heart?

Today Christ invites you to sit down at a charcoal fire

where he says, "Sit down. Guess how much I love you? Go ahead, guess . . . I hung on a cross with my arms wide-open, saying . . . I love you *this much!*"

You see, the father always loves you more.

PRAY FOR LOVE

I LOVE THE Travelocity commercial that has been running recently. An imperfect, but clearly ecstatic couple in desperate need of a tan relaxes on a tropical beach under palm trees, watching their kids build sand castles, when the wife blurts, "Our girl's amazing!"

The husband chimes in, "Our son's a genius."

Still beaming, the wife turns toward her husband, who obviously hasn't had a gym membership in years, and says, "You're amazing!"

To which he exclaims, "You look like a beach angel!"

She laughs hysterically.

Their enthusiastic passion for each other is infectious. It's irresistible. Travelocity, you've sold me.

Why can't Christians live like that?

Christians have been known for a lot of the wrong things. We've been known for being overopinionated, angry, judgmental, pious, and even discriminatory. We can change that.

What if instead of people knowing Christians for antagonizing, politicking, and protesting, they knew us for loving?

Knew us for pouring out a ridiculous amount of love on all who came near?

What if we actually became known for the beautiful things in the Bible, things that were most important to Christ? What if our light became so bright from living out the love of God that no one could miss it?

Here's what I'm getting at: God put you on earth to make it more like heaven.

When you say, "I forgive you"—you bring a bit of heaven to earth.

When you secretly pay your neighbor's rent when they've lost their job—you bring heaven to earth.

When you fly to Ethiopia and bring home an orphan—you bring heaven to earth.

When you invite a coworker to lunch, the one whom everyone avoids—you bring heaven to earth.

When you rescue a ten-year-old girl from a brothel in Phuket and enroll her in school—you bring heaven to earth.

When you swallow your criticism and complaints and instead make a habit of complimenting—you bring heaven to earth.

That is how God's will is done on earth, as it is in heaven.

It can be hard to love when there's so much hate all

around. So pray for love, and give your life to bringing the love of God from heaven to earth.

BE AMONG THEM

NOT LONG AFTER our family's bamboo-mat house burned in the jungle, a pastor from the Kru tribe, William Karmbleh, came from his village deep in the bush by the Atlantic to invite my parents to come and teach his people.

Knowing the place was remote, far from any road or town, my mother answered William, "How can we come? All our things have burned. We have no bedsheets to bring, no towels or soap, not even enough food."

His answer still rings in my ears, "Mother, we are human beings, too."

My parents agreed to go.

A few weeks later we made the trip to William's remote village by the beach. The Kru were incredibly gracious hosts. They had beds ready with clean sheets, they made their palm butter with fish for us at night, and best of all—and I still don't know how—they had doughnuts waiting in the morning!

Then my father built a small house in Baffu Bay so we could live among the Kru for months at a time and eat with them, worship with them, and know their names.

YOU CAN ONLY do so much from this side of the Atlantic, or the Pacific, or the Rio Grande. At some point you must go and be with the people you care about. None of us love so well from a distance.

If you are a church (a community of Christ-followers), let's say in Texas, then partner with a community in Rwanda. Don't scatter your resources by sending seventy-five dollars a month to people in fifteen different countries. Focus your energy and your effort. Become deeply acquainted with one people in one place before you spread or expand your reach. Pour your life, not just your money, into a community. They want your heart more than they want your shoes, or anything else you have to offer. They want to know you and know that you care.

OVER THE PAST ten years The Grove has grown a deep relationship with the Chimpampha community in Malawi. Last week Paul Gunther and our people were back among them again. At the end of a busy day just before sunset, one member of the tribe came to ask our team doctor if he would take a look at a paralyzed woman who was sick.

When Dr. John Hodgson first saw Kalinde he says he was stunned by her youth and beauty. Kalinde sat regally on a bamboo mat on the dirt in front of her mud hut. John's best guess was that TB had moved to her spine and destroyed the nerves, causing her paralysis.

Moving in closer to examine Kalinde his heart sank; he

knew she was dying. Her back and buttocks were one gaping tropical ulcer. The entire bottom half of her torso was decomposing. Bedsores, from sitting immobile on the ground, had ravaged her body, spread, and destroyed her flesh. Flies covered her wound and her face. Her bowels hung open and exposed. John says in all of his years of medical practice he has never seen a wound so severe.

After a few minutes of examining the massive sore, John shared the worst of the news. "There's nothing we can do." John knew there was not a hospital in the country that could perform the extensive skin grafts needed to save her life. He knew the infection was far too advanced, far too massive to reverse. John and his team left discouraged and feeling useless.

However, on their drive out of Chimpampha that evening, John said it suddenly hit him. "We *can* do something!"

Early the next morning John came back loaded with supplies. He said he may not be able to heal the sore that was killing Kalinde, but he and the others could give her love, comfort, and dignity. First they cleaned and dressed her gaping wounds and gave her medicine to make her more comfortable. Next the team moved her from the bamboo mat to a mattress they had bought earlier that morning. Then they hung a large mosquito net over Kalinde to keep the flies away and give her peace. They took away the shame and showed love as Christ loves.

Four days later Kalinde slipped away from her hell on earth and into heaven, where the Bible says, "There will be no more tears and no more pain."[6] There her sores will heal, and her legs will walk again.

Now the tribe at The Grove has joined with the Chechewa tribe of Chimpampha to build a clinic in Kalinde's name, so that sick young mothers will not die when they can live.

———

PAUL GUNTHER, ON our staff at The Grove, and his wife, Melinda, founded Live Love a few years ago. The sole purpose was to spread the everlasting love of Jesus Christ in our community, especially in our most blighted neighborhoods. Their volunteers tutor the children of immigrants, repaint fading houses, and refurbish overgrown yards. The message is always simple and clear: we love you in the same way Christ loves you.

Live Love just purchased a house in our community's most desperate neighborhood. It used to be a drug house; now we say it's a Jesus House. Interns will live there when the renovation is complete to serve and to love. The garage is being converted into an art studio. The living room is for music lessons and after-school tutoring. A dance team is already practicing in the driveway. And the dusty backyard is being tilled for a community garden.

The message that God loves is spreading in Chandler.

This fall our church set aside a day we called Live Love Sunday. On Live Love Sunday we focused on *being* the church instead of simply attending church.

Our invitation was for everyone—first-service people, second-service people, and third-service people—to meet at eight in the morning. Then we spread out into the neighborhoods and communities all around, hundreds and hundreds of people living the love of Jesus. We placed coffee cups on the front steps of a thousand of our neighbors' homes with a note inside that read, *Church service is canceled . . . so we can serve you.* We asked the people of The Grove to canvas their own neighborhoods to find people in need.

They refurbished homes of single mothers, cleaned local schools, weeded community gardens, did landscaping for widows, repaired broken plumbing, painted houses of grandmothers . . . and the list of eighty-two projects goes on.

Part of the impetus behind Live Love Sunday is the question I asked our people: "If, for some reason, we had to close the doors of our church and be gone forever, would our community miss us? Would they miss us because we have been so good for our neighborhoods? Would they miss us because something good and beautiful is happening here and it is leaking into the streets and homes of our city?"

I hope they would.

CONCLUSION
JOIN THE TRIBE

THE FUTURE CHURCH IS A tribe of passionate people. They have rejected the dispassion of the "evangelical" from decades past, who somehow missed the Bible's cry for justice, and equality, and dignity, and compassion, and beauty.

In striking contrast, the passions of Christ-followers today have taken a new and more meaningful direction. They have realized that the great godly purpose of the church is to take the kingdom of God to the world out there. That's God's dream for the earth. And only when we fully grasp this missional impetus of the Bible will people grow deep. Only when we realize the gospel is about filling this world with the beauty and love of God, and not just about making it into heaven, will people become healthy. Only when we encounter the heartbreak, affliction, and poverty of souls within the desperate people in broken places, will we understand the richness of knowing God.

This new church is a lot like a tribe. A *Barefoot Tribe*.

TOO OFTEN WE live with too low a view of our own lives. We think we can't make a difference. We believe the problems that plague this earth are too much for one person. But the Christ left this work of the kingdom to you. You must act.

I know without a doubt that God has planted a seed deep in your soul to change something that is not right in this world. You know what it is. It's different for each of us. For you, it may be to start an after-school art program in your city's most blighted neighborhood. Maybe you feel compelled to build homes for the refugees of war in Africa. Or you may become a voice for all the girls in the Middle East who are banned from attending school.

You know the special burden God has weighed on your heart. Maybe you have ignored it for years, thinking— hoping—it will fade. But it hasn't, has it?

The kind of life that pleases God, the Bible says, is to "Loose the chains of injustice, and untie the cords of the yoke, to set the oppressed free and break every yoke. Is it not to share your food with the hungry and to provide the poor wanderer with shelter—when you see the naked, to clothe them, and not to turn away from your own flesh and blood? Then your light will break forth like the dawn."[1]

God put you and me here to make this world a better place, a more beautiful place. Oppression, injustice, poverty, bigotry, and abuse are real and present. It doesn't have to be this way. When Jesus left, he asked that you and I continue to change and love the world.

Sometimes you must act to stop the very worst things from happening. You must stop the sex trade of girls in your city. You must stop the bigoted treatment of immigrants in your community. You must stop the racist talk in your office. You must stop the spread of AIDS in Africa.

And sometimes you must act in order for the very best things to happen. The best and the most beautiful things in life happen through God's people. It's a beautiful thing when you take off your shoes and slip them onto a woman's feet in Togo. It's a beautiful thing when you hang a mosquito net over a baby's bed in Zambia. It's a beautiful thing when you help a family rebuild their home after a tornado in Oklahoma. It's a beautiful thing when you bandage a child's tropical ulcer in Haiti. The world waits for you.

If I can only convince you of one thing, let me convince you that *you* are the one who will do the most critical things for God. Not for fame. Not to be spectacular, but to make this world better and more beautiful.

This is your invitation into the tribe of passionate people who have stopped waiting for somebody else to act. They are taking the initiative. They are launching the nonprofits, the NGOs, the new ministries to meet the needs they see around them. They are responding with passion to the causes God has weighed on their hearts.

It is easy to give your life to any number of things that don't matter a cent. You can give your life to watching too much TV. You can give your life to accumulating lots of great stuff like jet skis and snowboards. You can give your life to being popular and famous and spectacular. But at the end of the day, Jesus tells the affluent and powerful young man, none of this matters at all until you give your life away.

My invitation stands. Join us. This isn't like joining a political party, or a gym, or even a church. I invite you to a new way of life, a way to really live. I'm not asking for your money or your stuff . . .

God wants your life.

Will you innovate?

Will you speak up?

Will you step out?

Will you act?

Join the tribe.

www.JoinTheTribe.org

Acknowledgments

BOOKS ARE NEVER PUBLISHED WITHOUT help from brilliant, creative friends, colleagues, and family. This book is no exception. My deepest gratitude goes to:

Kathy Helmers, literary agent. Your inspiration is woven into the fabric of this book. I will forever be grateful for all your time and encouragement that has allowed me to be a writer.

Jim Chaffee, booking agent and tribal partner. Thank you for being such a trusted friend.

Jonathan Merkh, publisher. What a privilege to work with a fellow expatriate who sees that God is doing something good and beautiful in this world. Thank you for believing in the message of this book.

Becky Nesbitt, editor in chief. Your passion and enthusiasm are contagious. So good to work with a longtime friend.

Jessica Wong, editor. Thank you for your attention to detail and terrific ideas.

And the entire team at Howard Books/Simon & Schuster. You are the finest team any writer could ever want.

My wife, Veronica, and my four sons: Byron, Spencer, Christian, and William. Thank you for all your love and encouragement that fuels my life. There is nowhere else I would rather be than with you five. To my six brothers and sisters—Bill, Vann, Delbert, Lisa, Paul, and Marion—thank you for keeping me grounded. I love my big, crazy family.

To everyone at The Grove, Anthony Narducci, Paul Gunther, Josh Havens, Corey Conkright, Gary Bradley, Irving Mawolo, all my colleagues, elders, and friends, your relentless encouragement and support has been invaluable. I am so privileged to serve with a people who are utterly committed to the missional life God desires.

For Christ and his kingdom.

Notes

CHAPTER 1: Tribes

1. Jeremy Rifkin. *The Empathic Civilization: The Race to Global Consciousness in a World in Crisis.* Los Angeles: Tarcher, 2010.
2. Matthew 25:40 (author's paraphrase).

CHAPTER 2: The Barefoot Tribe

1. Seth Godin. *Tribes: We Need You to Lead Us.* New York: Portfolio, 2008.
2. John 13:14–17 (MSG).
3. Luke 4:17 (NLT).
4. Matthew 25 (author's paraphrase).

CHAPTER 3: Good News for Bare Feet

1. Luke 17:11–19.
2. Mark 5:29.

3. Mark 5:42.
4. Mark 1:45.
5. John Ortberg in a sermon titled "Silent Night." Menlo Park Presbyterian Church, December 15, 2001.
6. Much of my thinking on this subject of gospel has been profoundly influenced by Scot McKnight's *The King Jesus Gospel* and *One.Life*.

CHAPTER 4: A Tribal Kingdom

1. N. T. Wright. *The Challenge of Jesus*. Downers Grove, IL: IVP, 1999.
2. Scot McKnight. *One.Life*. Grand Rapids: Zondervan, 2010.
3. C. S. Lewis. *The Weight of Glory*. New York: HarperOne. 2009.
4. Matthew 6:10.
5. Matthew 3:2.
6. Matthew 10:7.
7. Luke 6:20–22.

CHAPTER 5: We Will Stop Injustice

1. Luke 16:14–31 (author's paraphrase).
2. Bono, remarks at the 54th National Prayer Breakfast, February 2, 2006. The Hilton Washington Hotel, Washington, DC.

CHAPTER 6: We Will Embrace People of Every Race, Nationality, and Background

1. Luke 14:23 (The Message).
2. Doug Stanglin. "Seniors Enjoy Ga. High School's First Integrated Prom." *USA Today*, April 29, 2013.
3. Matthew 25:35.
4. Luke 14:21.
5. Luke 14:12 (The Message).
6. Rachel Held Evans in *Letters to a Future Church*. Downers Grove: IVP, 2012.
7. Matthew 22:9 (CEV).
8. Matthew 5:43–44.
9. 2 Samuel 9:13.

CHAPTER 7: We Will Become
Social Entrepreneurs and Empower Fair Trade

1. Beverly Schwartz. *Rippling: How Entrepreneurs Spread Innovation Through the World*. San Francisco: Jossey-Bass, 2012.
2. 1 Corinthians 12:4–7.
3. Acts 2:44.
4. Dacher Keltner. "The Compassionate Species." "Greater Good Science Series." July 31, 2012. http://greatergood.berkeley.edu/article/item/the_compassionate_species.
5. William Drayton.
6. Scott McClellan. "Doing Good by Design." October 24, 2012. www.echohub.com.
7. Proverbs 13:23 (NLT).
8. Isaiah 58:3.
9. Mark Hensch. "Christian Fair Trade Group Gives the Poor a Fighting Chance." *Christian Post*. Friday, November 29, 2011.
10. "'Most Wanted' Corporate Human Rights Violators." By Global Exchange. www.globalexchange.org/corporateHRviolators.
11. "Child Labor Is Making a Disturbing Resurgence Around the World." *Business Insider*. January 2012. www.businessinsider.com.
12. James 5:2–5 (The Message).
13. Luke 4:18 (author's paraphrase).
14. Angela Petersen. "Activating the Vagus Nerve." *Exopermaculture*. October 12, 2012. http://exopermaculture.com/2013/07/03/the-vagus-nerve-biological-seat-of-compassion.
15. David Bornstein and Susan Davis. *Social Entrepreneurship: What Everyone Needs to Know*. New York: Oxford University Press, 2010.

CHAPTER 8: We Will Become Modern-Day Abolitionists

1. Chip Burrus, FBI Deputy Assistant Director. "Teen Girls' Stories of Sex Trafficking in U.S." *ABC News*. February 9, 2006. (Chip Burrus is founder of the Lost Innocence Project, which specializes in child and teen sex trafficking.)
2. Isaiah 58:6 (The Message).
3. Exodus 9:1.
4. Exodus 7:5 (NLT).
5. Exodus 9:16 (NLT).
6. Jason Newell. *Biola Magazine*. Spring 2012.

CHAPTER 9: We Will End Extreme Poverty

1. Jeffrey Sachs. *The End of Poverty: Economic Possibilities for Our Time*. New York: Penguin Books, 2006. 289.
2. Matthew 25:31–46.
3. Matthew 5:40.
4. Luke 16.
5. Luke 18:22.
6. William Easterly, professor of economics, New York University. Recorded July 6, 2007. http://bigthink.com/ideas/5035.
7. These suggestions are rooted in Jeffrey Sachs's *The End of Poverty*.
8. Steve Corbett and Brian Fikkert. *When Helping Hurts*. Chicago: Moody Press, 2009.
9. Anna Yukhananov. "World Bank Moves Up Deadline for Ending Extreme Poverty by 10 Years." Reuters. October 9, 2013.
10. Scott Todd. Fast Living–58. Colorado Springs: Compassion. 2011. Location 474–491.

CHAPTER 10: We Will Stop the Spread of Pandemics

1. Laurie Lathem. "Turning Passion into Action." *Wiretap Magazine*. October 22, 2008.
2. Bill Gates. "Malaria Eradication." Reuters, October 18, 2011.
3. "NE Launches Cutting Edge PSA 'No Child Born with HIV by 2015.'" ONE press release. Washington, DC, and New York. www.one.org/us/press/one-launches-cutting-edge-psa-no-child-born-with-hiv-by-2015.
4. "Eradication of Malaria Is in Sight." *Medical News Today*. September 12, 2011.
5. Jenny Trinitapoli and Alexander Weinreb. "Good News on AIDS in Africa." *Medical Examiner*. March 27, 2013.
6. Netting Nations. www.NettingNations.org.

CHAPTER 11: We Will Put Down Our Weapons

1. Matthew 5:39.
2. Luke 6:27–28.
3. Matthew 26:52.
4. Anderson speaks exclusively with Sergio Consuegra. October 5, 2013. www.youtube.com/watch?v=GoHEgz5-tUA.

5. Dave Urbanski. "Witness Was on His Way to Church When He Saw Enraged Biker Gang Attacking Family in SUV—What He Did Next Should Inspire Us All." *The Blaze.* October 6, 2013.
6. Psalm 121:7.
7. Romans 8:28.
8. Psalms 115:3 (The Message).
9. Isaiah 2:4.
10. Edna Fernandes. "Face to Face with General Butt Naked: 'The Most Evil Man in the world.'" *Mail.* November 27, 2010.

CHAPTER 12: We Will Promote Sustainability and Care for the Environment

1. Lynn White. *The Historical Roots of Our Ecological Crisis.* 1967.
2. Tony Compolo. *How to Rescue the Earth Without Worshiping Nature.* Nashville: Thomas Nelson, 1992.
3. Ian Cron, 2006. Chasing Francis: A Pilgrim's Tale. Colorado Springs: NavPress, 2006. 45.
4. A widely accepted definition of sustainability comes from the 1987 UN conference.
5. Ian Morgan Cron.
6. Ibid.
7. Wendee Holtcamp. "Back to Eden: Students Find Inspiration in Creation Care." The American Scientific Affiliation. www.asa3.org/ASA/topics/Youth%20Page/enviro1.htm.
8. Jonathan Merritt. "Green Plus Christian Isn't New Math." *Christianity Today.* June 30, 2010.
9. Genesis 1:26 (The Message).

CHAPTER 13: We Will Live Simply

1. The full story of Jim Knuppe's pioneering work in the self-storage business is told in this biography: Marc Grossman. *The Jim Knuppe Story.* Bloomington: Author House, 2009.
2. Ecclesiastes 2:18 (NIV).
3. Matthew 6:19–21 (NLT).
4. Dave Ramsey interviews Mike Foster, founder and president of the Junky Car Club. Fox Business News. May 6, 2011.
5. Psalm 24:1 (NIV).
6. Luke 18:22 (author's paraphrase).

7. Luke 6:38 (The Message).
8. Acts 20:35 (NLT).

CHAPTER 14: We Will Create More Art
and Make the World Beautiful

1. Leonard Sweet. *Soul Salsa*. Grand Rapids: Zondervan, 2002.
2. Donald Miller. *Searching for God Knows What*. Nashville: Thomas Nelson, 2004, 53–55.
3. From Song of Songs 4:1, 9–11 (NIV).
4. Psalm 144:9 (NIV).

CHAPTER 15: We Will Love Like Christ—Always

1. Isaiah 58:3–4.
2. From Mark 12:30–31.
3. 1 Corinthians 13:13.
4. Sam McBratney. *Guess How Much I Love You*. Sommerville, MA: Candlewick Press. 2008.
5. These thoughts on love are inspired by John Ortberg. In my opinion, no other contemporary Christian writer grasps the idea of the love of God like John Ortberg. I am a different person for reading his thoughts about God. For a start, see Ortberg's *Love Beyond Reason*. Grand Rapids: Zondervan, 2001.
6. Revelation 21:4 (author's paraphrase).

CONCLUSION: Join the Tribe

1. Isaiah 58:6–7.

About the Author

PALMER CHINCHEN, PHD, IS LEAD pastor of The Grove in Chandler, Arizona, a young, innovative, and rapidly growing congregation. Before that he served as a college pastor at Wheaton Bible Church in Wheaton, Illinois, and at Biola University in La Mirada, California.

Palmer was raised deep in the jungle of Liberia, where the only way in and out was by prop plane. He later returned to Africa with his wife, Veronica, and four sons, where he taught spiritual development and practical theology at African Bible College in Malawi and Liberia.

A rising voice in the missional movement, Palmer is passionate about creating a fresh desire among Christians to reach a hurting world. Drawing from his experiences growing up in Africa, Palmer writes and speaks with authority about the most desperate needs facing our world today. His memories of the ravages of war and disease, as well as the effects of extreme poverty, fuel his desire to see us change what is not right in our world.

About ten years ago Palmer moved with his family to the booming Phoenix East Valley city of Chandler to help grow a one-year-old church plant. Over Palmer's time at The Grove, the church has experienced exponential growth and a tribe of Christ-followers has gathered who tirelessly work together to stop injustice, end extreme poverty, and share the love of Christ.

Palmer holds a PhD in educational studies from Trinity Evangelical Divinity School in Illinois and a BA and MA in intercultural student from Biola University in California.

BAREFOOT
TRIBE

OCT. 16th–18th, 2014

PHX - AZ
at The GROVE, in Chandler

You are invited to join a gathering of cultural artists and social entrepreneurs committed to justice, sustainability, art, compassion, austerity, and spreading the love of God. The aim of the GATHERING is to promote conversation and collaboration that will inspire this generation of innovators to pool their best wisdom, abilities, and passion to make the world as good and as beautiful as God intended.

REGISTER today at
www.BarefootTribe.com
or call:
480.883.7600

GATHERING

FEATURED VOICES

ERWIN McManus
Futurist, artist, filmmaker, author, storyteller, activist, and innovator, Erwin inspires each person to live their most heroic life and advance the common good through the power of story, beauty, and design.

BOB Goff
Compelling communicator and author of the *New York Times* bestseller, *Love Does*, Bob is an attorney passionate about justice and turning the tide on extreme poverty.

RACHEL Held Evans
With more than a quarter of a million visits to her blog each month Rachel has become a fresh voice for the next generation church, challenging its marginalization of women and dispassion toward justice.

Along with **Palmer Chinchen** and a crowd of innovative thinkers who will speak and lead seminars on justice, social entrepreneurship, and compassion.

Worship Led by **Josh Havens** (The Afters)